CAR
TALK

WITH
CLICK
AND
CLACK
THE
TAPPET
BROTHERS

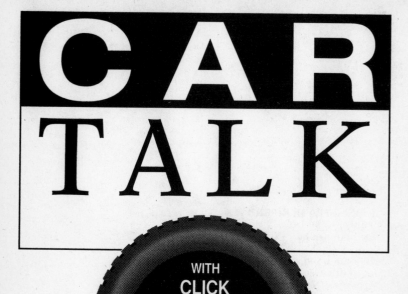

CAR TALK

WITH
CLICK
AND
CLACK
THE
TAPPET
BROTHERS

Tom and Ray Magliozzi
with Terry Bisson

Illustrated by Harry Trumbore

A DELL TRADE PAPERBACK

A DELL TRADE PAPERBACK
Published by
Dell Publishing
a division of
Bantam Doubleday Dell Publishing Group, Inc.
666 Fifth Avenue
New York, New York 10103

ISBN: 0-440-50364-7

Design: Stanley S. Drate/Folio Graphics Co. Inc.

Printed in the United States of America

Published simultaneously in Canada

April 1991

10 9 8 7 6 5 4 3 2 1

RRH

ACKNOWLEDGMENTS

Every book has acknowledgments, and it should be so. After all, just because a few people's names appear on the cover, are *they* the only ones responsible for the book's existence?

Yes.

Except maybe for Theresa Agrillo, the poor woman who had to listen to thousands (maybe billions!) of our radio shows so she could type up the transcripts. Talk about punishment.

DISCLAIMER

Names, details, and origins of phone calls have been changed to protect the innocent. Not to mention the guilty.

CONTENTS

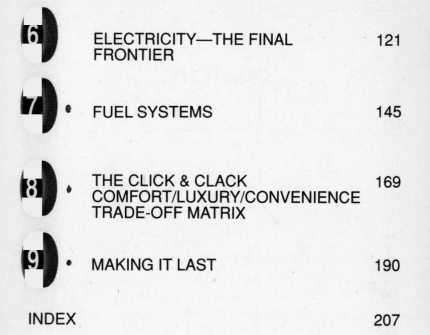

INTRODUCTION

Aren't cars a pain in the butt?

You know, compared to a TV set or a microwave oven. You turn on the TV and it either works or it doesn't. If it doesn't, you make sure that it's plugged in and the fuse isn't blown. If it still doesn't work, you can call someone to fix it and he tells you that it's cheaper to buy a new one, so you throw it away, and that's the end of that. Easy.

But a car! Jeez. You're married to the damn thing. Sometimes you wish you could just throw it away, but you're still making payments to the bank (or to that sleazeball brother-in-law who's charging you 25 percent interest, and you *know* he's connected to the mob, so you can't stiff him).

We even stuck you for $10.00 to buy this book! Is there no justice?

Well, it may not be as bad as all that. In fact, you might actually *save* some money by reading this book. We hope to tell you enough about how your car works so that (A) you won't get ripped off by unscrupulous or unknowledgeable repair shops; (B) you won't make bad (or at least uninformed) decisions about how to treat your car; and (C) you won't dump your car prematurely. ("We will junk no car before its time.")

This book is so simple that even an auto mechanic can understand it. The first chapter will give you a kind of big picture about what cars are made of and what the pieces do. We have cleverly titled this chapter The Big Picture.

In subsequent chapters, we take a few pages to describe the purpose and function of various important systems (such as the cooling system or the brakes), and then we throw in some of the phone calls we've received on our National Public Radio program from our "billions of listeners" (I think actually eight listeners—all relatives). We thought this would be an interesting approach since:

(A) These are real problems from real people.
(B) They enable us to draw on our vast wealth of practical experience.
(C) It made it a hell of a lot easier to write the book.

Please be sure to read the book carefully and underline the items of interest with a ballpoint pen. That way, if you like the book and decide to give a copy to a friend, you'll have to *buy* another copy. This will add another twenty-five or thirty cents to our favorite charity, the Save the Skeets Foundation. We discovered a few years ago that people were shooting skeets, which are fast becoming an endangered species. They're such cute little guys that we can't understand how anyone could shoot them. In any event, all proceeds from this book will go to the foundation.

If, on the other hand, you don't like the book for some reason, then don't tell us. Just write to the *Car Talk* Hate Mail Division, care of our attorneys, Dewey, Cheatem, and Howe. Then go out and shoot a skeet. They're disgusting little creatures anyway.

CAR TALK

WITH
CLICK
AND
CLACK
THE
TAPPET
BROTHERS

1

THE BIG
PICTURE

This is a little picture of the big picture.

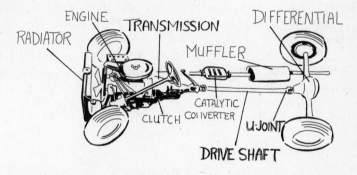

These are most of the major pieces (or systems) of a car. This particular diagram shows a *rear-wheel-drive* car, which means that the rear wheels provide the power to push the vehicle. Actually, most modern cars are *front-wheel drive*—that is, the front wheels provide the power to pull the car. It happens to be easier to show all the pieces and explain what they do by using the rear-wheel-drive configuration, because in front-wheel drive all the pieces are crammed in together under the hood. If we tried to draw all these pieces using the front-wheel-drive configuration, it would look something like this:

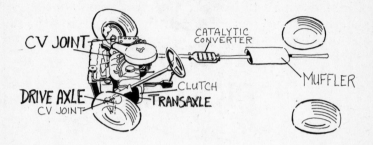

This one is difficult to explain, even to our therapist. Actually, all cars—front- *or* rear-wheel drive—have basically the same pieces. So once you understand the rear-wheel-drive version, you'll also understand the front-wheel-drive version. We'll use diagram 1 to explain what all the pieces do; then you'll have what? Right! The Big Picture!

You may already know a lot of what's explained in this chapter, but so what? The fact that you are a regular listener to our show (you are, aren't you?) indicates that you aren't very particular about how you spend your time. So read it anyway. What the heck.

THE ENGINE

Just to show you that this is really a *big* picture, we're going to reduce the entire engine to one piece. Because almost the only purpose of all the parts and systems that make up the engine is to spin a shaft. It's called the crankshaft, and only a short piece of it sticks out of the engine at each end.

This shaft spins, and the rotation of this shaft ultimately results in the rotation of the wheels, which in turn makes the car move. Simple, huh?

Just to give you a feel for how the crankshaft spins, think of a bicycle. Here's an exploded view of the pedals of a bike, a pair of feet and the piece that connects the pedals to each other. Your feet push down and the up-and-down motion of your feet makes that piece in the middle turn. See it in the drawing?

THIS PIECE TURNS

EXPLODED VIEW

The piece labeled "this piece turns" is the crankshaft of the bicycle, and what happens on a bike is about the same thing that happens in a car—except that in the car the crankshaft is heavier and longer; sort of like this:

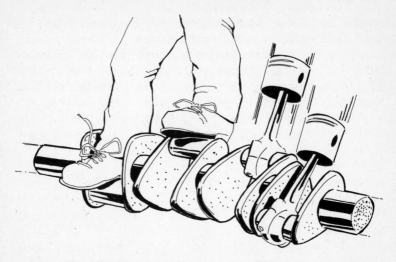

In the engine, the pedals are replaced by things called pistons, which are inside cylinders, and the power of your feet is replaced by explosions taking place above the pistons, pushing the pistons down. This downward motion of the pistons makes the crankshaft rotate, just like the downward push of your feet makes the crankshaft of the bike rotate. (In the car, there are usually more feet: four-cylinder engines have four pistons, or four feet pushing; six-cylinder engines have six.)

We'll talk more about the details of the engine later (in fact, we'll tell you exactly what's inside it), but for now just think of it as a device with a crankshaft that spins; the faster you pedal (or step on the gas and make the force of the explosions greater), the faster the shaft spins.

THE CLUTCH

The only problem with the arrangement described above is that if you connected this spinning shaft directly to the wheels, then whenever the engine was running, the wheels would want to turn. You'd have to turn off the engine every time you came to a red light and then turn it on again when you wanted to continue. That's no way to drive. (It works okay with the bike, though. The next time you're riding a bike and you come to a stop sign, glance down at your feet. You'll notice that they aren't moving! The engine is off.)

Anyway, rather than turning the engine on and off, it's better if we have a way of disconnecting the spinning shaft from everything else when we're stopped and then reconnecting it when we're ready to go. The piece that reconnects the crankshaft to the rest of the car (and ultimately to the wheels) is the *clutch*. And how does it do this? It *grabs on to*—yes, actually clutches!—the end of the crankshaft.

Let's suppose you get turned on by spinning your brains into jelly. Here's the engine with the crankshaft spinning, and here's my brother with his usual stupid grin on his face.

Okay. He's ready to go. He grabs (clutches) the crankshaft and away he goes.

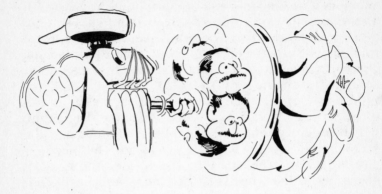

Now he's ready to blow his lunch. All he needs to do is let go, or disengage the clutch. (Actually, maybe this is a good idea for a ride at an amusement park. I can see it now—"Tappetland"; but I digress.) When your foot is on the clutch, it's disengaged, and when it's off the clutch, it's engaged.

The reason you don't have to do all this with an automatic transmission is that a piece called a *torque converter* does it for you. In other words, an automatic transmission also includes an automatic clutch.

THE TRANSMISSION

As you probably know, there are two kinds of transmissions, automatic and manual, sometimes called "standard." In both cases, the purpose of the transmission is to make a trade-off between power and speed, because you (usually) can't have both. Sometimes you'd rather have power, like when you're starting off. Then you need power because you're trying to move a ton or two of iron from a dead stop. (This is one of those Laws of Motion; something about if Isaac Newton is resting, he wants to keep resting.)

Once the car is moving, however, it's easier to keep it

moving. If you're doubtful about this, try pushing a car. Better yet, if you're resting and would like to continue resting, watch some other people pushing a car. It takes two or three gorilla lookalikes with a lot of grunting and groaning to get it moving; but once it *is* moving, a little milquetoast guy can come along and keep it going with one hand.

The transmission has gears inside it that make this trade-off between power and speed. The motion of the spinning crankshaft goes into the front of the transmission, and out the back of the transmission comes another shaft that is either spinning (relatively) slowly with lots of power (low gear for starting off) or spinning faster with less power (high gear for tooling down the highway).

With a manual transmission (your basic stick shift) you change the gears yourself. The automatic transmission does it for you—automagically!

THE DRIVE SHAFT AND UNIVERSAL JOINTS

Okay. We now have a shaft spinning at the right speed and with the right amount of power. Now we have to get this spinning motion to the back wheels by extending the shaft; that's all the *drive shaft* is—an extension of the spinning shaft coming out of the transmission.

The only problem with extending the shaft is that the car bounces up and down while you drive, and the front and back of the car don't always bounce up and down in unison (your front wheels hit a pothole and a second later your back wheels hit the same pothole). A perfectly rigid shaft would bend or break, so we have to let the drive shaft flex. This is done with devices called *universal joints*, which are attached to each end of the drive shaft, and sometimes to the middle too.

Since most mechanics are unwilling to pronounce words of so many syllables, these are referred to as "U joints." In the front-wheel-drive configuration, these

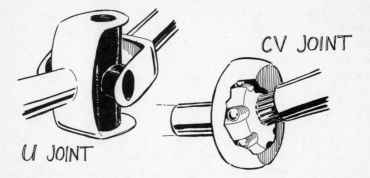

CV JOINT

U JOINT

things are in the front and are called *constant velocity joints*. (That's right. You figured that out right away! Mechanics call them "C-V joints.") They're set up differently—and naturally, more expensively!—but they accomplish essentially the same thing. (The word "essentially" has been used to weasel out of really explaining the difference, which is beyond the scope of a low-tech book like this. If you really have to know, look for the high-tech sequel, *Son of Car Talk*, available at your bookstore soon.)

THE REAR END (I BEG YOUR PARDON)

You may notice that the shaft is spinning in the wrong direction; the way it's going, the car would move sideways.

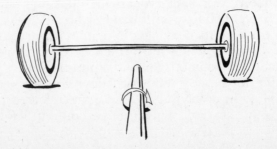

This is illegal in many states (though not necessarily in California), so we need to convert the motion from sideways to forward. This is quite easy to do with a couple of gears.

But the more important reason for the *differential* is to allow one of the driving wheels to turn faster than the other. Think about what happens when you turn a corner. The inside wheel has to turn slower than the outside wheel; otherwise it would slide or skid or who knows what.

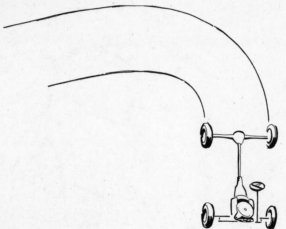

That's it. That's the Big Picture. It's so simple that we're almost embarrassed to take your money. (I said *almost.*)

FRONT-WHEEL DRIVE VS. REAR-WHEEL DRIVE VS.
FOUR-WHEEL DRIVE VS. . . . .

All the pieces that we've described above constitute what's called the *drivetrain*—the engine, clutch, transmission, drive shaft, rear end (differential), and axles. But there are other ways to configure them. For example, you could put all of it in the rear and drive (provide power to) the rear wheels. That would be a "rear-engine, rear-wheel-drive" car, the most famous of which was the VW Beetle and the most infamous, the Chevy Corvair. Of course, this arrangement gets rid of the need for the drive shaft.

Or you could put it all up front and have—aha! front-wheel drive. Put the engine in sideways, combine the transmission and differential in one *transaxle*, and you have what has become a very common configuration for both foreign and domestic cars. Now the front wheels provide the power and the rear wheels just go along for the ride.

A FRENCH CAR - CITROËN 2CV

I suppose you could also put the engine in the rear and have it drive the front wheels. Nobody has ever done this, to our knowledge. If anyone ever did, it was probably the French. (Click and Clack Rule Number 122—"Nobody copies the French, and the French don't copy anybody.")

SO WHAT?

What are the real differences among all these configurations? Is one of them intrinsically better than all others? Well, there are really two major considerations. One is *traction*, and the other has to do with whether you can cram ten pounds of stuff into a five-pound bag.

First, traction. When you step on the gas, does the car go? Or do the wheels just spin? If the car goes, you have traction. Traction is good (unless you've had an accident and you're *in* traction). All things being equal, the amount of traction you get is a function of how much weight is *over* the wheels that are powering the car. And other things being equal, the worst arrangement is to have the heavy parts of the car at one end and the driving wheels at the other—to have the engine in the front and the driving wheels in the rear. The best configuration, actually, is to have the engine in the middle of the car; or (if you can't spare the passenger seat) to have everything either up front (like a Honda or a Saab) or out back (like a VW bug or a Corvair).

This might suggest that the front-wheel-drive cars that are now so popular are really better. A thinking person might then ask, "Why did it take a hundred years to figure that out?"

Go ahead. Ask.

I'm glad you asked! Here's the answer. Where you put the engine and the driving wheels doesn't make *all* that much difference *unless* you make a car that's too light to begin with. I mean, for the first one hundred years of making cars, they mostly had the engine in the front and the driving wheels in the back. Until the fuel crisis of the 1970s. Then, everyone made cars smaller to improve gas mileage, and pretty soon they were too small to have enough traction, so front-wheel drive (FWD) became the fad.

It has a lot to do with size. As proof of this, ask why aren't the following cars FWD: Chevy Caprice, Ford Crown Victoria, Mercedes, Volvo, Mazda 929? Or the best example, garbage trucks?

Because they're *heavy enough*. Even "little" cars were mostly *rear-wheel drive* in the old days: MG, Triumph, Alfa Romeo. But if you make the car *really* light, it's almost undriveable—especially in snow. So to make a small car with the engine in the front driveable, you almost *have* to make it front-wheel drive!

Does that make it better? Here's a test I did last winter. There it was, snowing like heck, and I happened to have, parked in my driveway, a VW Jetta and a Lincoln Town Car. The Jetta is front-wheel drive and weighs about 2,300 pounds. The Town Car is rear-wheel drive and weighs 4,000 pounds. I took them both out for a test drive to compare traction for going and traction for stopping. The Lincoln was much better than the Jetta. The wheels didn't spin taking off from a stop and didn't skid when coming to a stop. The Jetta wasn't bad. But the Lincoln Town Car was better.

So where does that leave you poor turkeys who can't afford a Lincoln (or drive a customer's home)? First of all, if it doesn't snow where you live and you stay out of the mud, your primary consideration doesn't have to be traction. You might want to consider, however, the second factor (besides traction) that we alluded to a couple of pages ago: How much stuff can you cram into that five-pound bag? Because part of the reason that cars were made the way they were made (engine in the front, rear wheels driving) is that it made it easier to *fix* them. When you cram *everything* under the hood, then everything is in the way of everything else. This means that it's harder and takes longer and costs more money to fix a front-wheel-drive car. (Actually, they're getting better. It used to be impossible. Now it's only a pain in the butt.)

So, should you buy front-wheel drive or rear-wheel drive? Gee, I don't care. Are you in love with the looks of Hondas (front-wheel drive)? Fine. Have you just fallen head over heels for a Mustang convertible (rear-wheel drive)? Fine too. We'll make more money fixing the Honda; but then, someone has to pay for all our trips to Hawaii.

An issue that *is* important, though, is *how small* a car should you buy. This is, of course, a matter of opinion, and if you have an opinion that conflicts with ours, then write your own book. But here's ours, and the impeccable logic from which it derives.

It seems to us that a car ought to weigh more than a horse—a lot more. God made horses and a horse can run at about 35 miles per hour. A big horse weighs about 1,500 pounds. Most people want to drive at about 70 miles per hour. So, a vehicle that can go 70 m.p.h. ought to weigh 70/35, or twice as much as a horse. Everybody knows this. It is a universal constant. It is God's Law.

This means that cars that *can* travel at 70 m.p.h. *must* weigh 3,000 pounds. That's it. (Yes, we know that a jaguar—the animal, not the car—can run at 70 miles per hour; and as proof of God's Law, no one has ever driven or ridden on the back of a jaguar—the animal, not the car. For that matter, not many people have ever driven a Jaguar—the car, not the animal.)

If you want to save the environment and/or you want to save money on gas, don't do it by buying a car that's so small that it will kill you. Just don't drive so much.

The last issue. Four-wheel drive. In 4WD, all four wheels are driven. Mostly, they start out as rear-wheel drive and another "box" called a transfer case sends power to the front wheels as well as the rear ones.

Should you buy 4WD? Jeez. I don't know. Are you an obstetrician in Antarctica? Do you chase goats up the sides of mountains? Is your self-esteem directly related to your ability to drive around in deep snow? If the answer to these questions is yes, you need 4WD. But if you drive on ordinary city streets that are usually plowed, then why would you want 4WD?

Lastly, most of the vehicles that are 4WD are not *cars*. They are utility vehicles that sit high off the ground and have short wheelbases, both of which tend to make them unstable. In fact, these vehicles have a mandatory warning label pasted to the dashboard that clearly states: WARNING! THIS IS NOT A CAR. DON'T DRIVE IT LIKE A CAR OR YOU WILL SURELY DIE. IF YOU DIE, THEN NO ONE WILL BE AROUND WHO IS STUPID ENOUGH TO BUY NEXT YEAR'S MODEL.

Or something like that.

2

SHIMMIES AND SHAKES

There are three kinds of problems you can have with your car: (1) those that will kill you; (2) those that will leave you stranded; and (3) those that will cost you more money if you let them go too long.

Most transmission and engine problems come under category two. Battery problems, starters that don't start, fuel injectors that don't inject, whining transmissions, clanking universal joints are also category two. These can also be life threatening if you commute from Alaska or drive an ambulance, but for the most part they are less serious than category one.

Category three endangers primarily your pocketbook. It includes engine problems such as noisy tappets that click and clack, engine knocks, stuff like that.

Shimmies and shakes—problems that have to do with the suspension and steering of your car—*all* come under category one. So we're going to look at them in some detail.

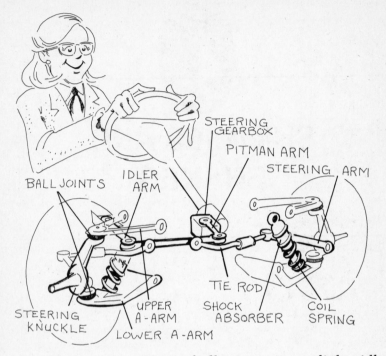

STEERING GEARBOX

PITMAN ARM

STEERING ARM

BALL JOINTS

IDLER ARM

STEERING KNUCKLE

UPPER A-ARM

LOWER A-ARM

SHOCK ABSORBER

TIE ROD

COIL SPRING

The steering pieces—ball joints, center links, idler arms, Pitman arms, drag links, tie-rod ends, and so forth—literally hold the front wheels to the rest of the car. If any one of these things breaks, you're in serious trouble. And so is anybody else on the road in your vicinity. Since this might include us, or even our radio listeners, we take this seriously.

You might say, well, there's nothing I can do about it. If they're going to break, they're going to break. Wrong! If you know what to look for, you can heed early warning signals.

A funny thing happens. People never know when their car is handling badly, because all the things that wear out generally wear out slowly, or incrementally, as the mathematicians say. Every day, the car gets a little worse—the ball joints get a little looser, the tie-rod ends get a little sloppier, your tires get a little squarer, and all kinds of things happen to make the car handle worse. Except you don't notice because the changes are so small that you adapt to them.

I'll tell you a little story. A customer brought a car into the garage once and asked us to drive it at high speed to listen for a noise it was making at 60 m.p.h. I took the car out on the highway and by the time I got it up to 60 my heart was in my throat. This thing kept changing lanes without notice. I would turn the wheel a little bit, the car wouldn't respond. I turned it a little bit more and all of a sudden it shot over into the next lane, back and forth. Anyway, I never got to hear the noise because I was so scared.

I told the customer about it when he came back and he looked at me like I was crazy. I went for a ride with him driving because I wanted to hear the noise, plus I was curious to see how he was able to handle the car.

Well, he drove at 60 as if there were nothing to it. He was as cool as a cucumber, while his hand on the steering wheel would go back and forth from three o'clock to nine o'clock and back to three o'clock. And, of course, all the time he was doing this, the car was going in a straight line.

The reason he could handle the thing so well was that as the steering components got more and more worn out, and the car handled worse and worse every day, he had gradually adapted to it. So he was able to keep this junkbox on the road, whereas I, who was accustomed to driving a car that had reasonably tight steering, was at a loss.

When we finally put it up on the lift and checked it, he had tie-rod ends that were ready to fall off because their ball-and-socket joints had all worn out; and ball joints that hadn't been greased in a hundred years; and so forth. The car was an accident waiting to happen.

This fellow's case was extreme, but not so unusual. Most people don't do anything to fix their cars unless something awful happens. The car begins to shake when you're driving at high speed and you just slow down a little—or maybe even go faster! Or maybe you think, "When I get new tires it'll take care of itself."

But there are a lot of other things besides bad tires that can cause high-speed vibrations. For example, bad ball joints or bad tie-rod ends can cause this problem. And a worn-out ball joint or tie-rod end is apt to break if you hit something like a pothole at high speed.

So don't wait until the rattling in the car is so bad that the change keeps falling out of your pockets. A good suggestion is to have someone else drive your car, someone who's accustomed to driving a car that's not as much of a jalopy. Preferably, your mechanic.

You might drive another car yourself, one that's in better shape than your own. If you find yourself thinking, "Jeez, this car doesn't dart to the left when I turn the wheel to the right, like mine does. What's the matter with it?" you might learn something about your own car.

One good thing about today's smaller cars that wasn't the case with the Imperial Starcruisers of yesteryear is that ball joints and tie-rod ends don't wear out at anywhere near the rate they used to. The reason for this is that they have to make these pieces a certain minimum size. If a modern car is half the weight a car was fifteen years ago, they can't necessarily make the critical parts half the size—they have to be at least big enough not to bend double when you hit potholes and drive into curbs. So in a sense, these parts are really extra-heavy duty, and it's not unusual to see smaller cars with tie-rod ends and ball joints that are in perfect condition after 100,000 miles.

In other words, don't be afraid to have them looked at. You might be pleasantly surprised.

YOU'RE SUSPENDED!

Everyone knows what the steering mechanism is responsible for—it points you toward the mall, and back toward home. But this notion of suspension is less obvious.

The suspension is the mechanism that suspends, or isolates, you from the road. In other words, it comes between the tires that ride on the road and the part of your anatomy that connects with the driver's seat. When you hit a bump in the road, you don't want that bump telegraphed through a rigid chassis right up into the seat of your pants the way it did with the buckboards of old, because it becomes uncomfortable to have your head banging around against the roof. It also makes it difficult to keep the car under control.

So the suspension, as its name implies, suspends the passengers in their passenger compartment and isolates them (at least partially) from the bumps of the road. The parts that are responsible for this are primarily the springs and shock absorbers. When they wear out, they can affect the handling of the car in a serious way.

Springs almost never wear out,* so the only suspension parts you really have to worry about are the shock absorbers. For those of you who have McPherson struts— they're nothing more than springs and shocks in one unit (and are more expensive to replace!).

When your car hits a bump, the springs absorb the energy of the impact by getting compressed. Now, the problem with springs is that they are springy. They keep springing. That's what makes a pogo stick work. But what's good for Pogo isn't necessarily good for your car. So you have shock absorbers, which are like those little things that keep screen doors from slamming. The shock absorbers slow the oscillations of the springs so that the car doesn't go down the road bouncing up and down repeatedly after hitting every bump.

You can see now that these things have really been

---

*Unless you consistently carry lots of heavy stuff—cinder blocks, for example. Or unless you, yourself, are heavy stuff. If so, springs *will* wear out—that is, lose their springiness.

misnamed! All of America knows them as shock absorbers. But what really absorbs the shock is the spring. The shock absorber should really be called a *damper,* since it prevents the spring from going *boing, boing, boing.* (Get it? The springs absorb the shock and the shocks dampen the springing. And you wonder why you've been confused.)

The shocks, in addition to making the ride more comfortable, are also there to prevent the tires from bouncing excessively on the road. If your shocks are bad, your tires will not be making what we call point-for-point contact with the road. In fact, there will be times when they are actually jumping off the road surface, because the springs pull up as well as compress down.

It can get a little tricky handling a car when the front tires are not touching the ground half the time, especially on wet roads. So the shock absorbers are there to keep the tires planted on the pavement. In other words, they are as critical to safety as to comfort.

Drive alongside some jalopy that you know probably hasn't had its shocks changed in 100,000 miles. (Or if you own the jalopy, have somebody else drive while you watch from another car.) Watch the front tires and you'll see them bouncing all over the road like Curly Neil dribbling a basketball. They're not hugging the road—they're bouncing off it, and the car isn't handling well, to say the least.

Then look at another car that has good shock absorbers, a car that's maybe a year or so old, and you'll see that those tires are actually following every little contour and dip and rise in the road. They're hugging the road. That car handles a lot better, and of course, it has a better ride, but that's just secondary. The handling and the tracking are what you're really after, and that's why the shocks are so important.

One interesting note about shock absorbers. If you've had your shocks for 50,000 miles and you think they haven't worn out, you're wrong. There's no way shocks or struts can last more than 50,000 miles unless you're driving on supersmooth superhighways all the time. If you're driving, like the rest of us, on city streets or country roads that are bumpy and lumpy, you'll have ruined the shocks by 50,000 miles or sooner. You just won't know it, because they got a little bit worse every day.

The same thing is true of your tires. If you got 50K out of those cheap tires they put on the car when it was new, you've really accomplished something. And chances are, if you look carefully, you can see the air inside the tires by then. So get rid of them. Get baby some new shoes.

You might even like the car again. You liked it when you bought it, and if you've fallen out of love with it, maybe a brand-new set of super-duper tires will help you to fall back in love with it. New tires and new shocks can do a lot. It's almost like getting a paint job.

One thing you can do, even though most people don't ever do it, is check your tire pressure. Why? Because the correct tire pressure will help the car ride better, as well as hold the road better, and correctly inflated tires last longer.

Checking the tires also gives you a good opportunity to actually take a *look* at your tires. You can see if the tread is wearing nice and evenly. See if there are any areas that are cupped or if the inside edge or the outside edge is worn out. Look for these things because that's going to alert you to problems. If your alignment is way off or you have bad struts or bad shocks that are causing the tires to wear out peculiarly, it'd be nice to get this stuff taken care of before you ruin a perfectly good set of tires.

Don't bother with those little tire pressure gauges that look like chrome pens—the ones that always say you have 40 pounds of air in the tire when you really have 20, or more often vice versa. Don't ever trust the things at the filling stations either. Those are notoriously inaccurate. If you really want to get a tire pressure gauge, get one of the round ones. They're not much more expensive and they look classy. Everyone'll be impressed, plus you'll get an accurate reading.

When you check your tire pressure, you should always do it with the tires cold. If it's summer, you can keep them in the refrigerator overnight. (Just kidding. Tires get hot when you drive because of the friction between the tread and the road, so "cold" just means a tire you haven't driven very far on.)

Here are a few questions that were called in to our radio show. If you've been paying attention so far, you should be able to figure out the answers. We almost did.

Let's Go to the Hop

I have a question about brakes.

CLICK: Okay, shoot.

At least I think it's about brakes. I drive to work every day on the freeway and there's this one exit where there's a stop sign at the end of a very short exit ramp. Sometimes I have to make a very quick, hard stop in a short distance.

CLACK: And your car does the hop.

Well, yes, it bounces up and down as if there were ripples in the road.

CLACK: There probably are.

CLICK: Try it on another road.

Yeah, I did, and it did. Is this the brakes?

CLICK: Not directly. It doesn't take very much of a washboard to make a car behave peculiarly on braking, because you change the weight distribution when you brake. The car pitches forward as you apply pressure to the brakes, and all the weight goes forward. My guess is that you have a rear-wheel-drive car. Right?

Nope. It's a front-wheel-drive Toyota Tercel, a wagon.

CLACK: My brother scores again.

CLICK: Well, it's possible that the back wheels are the ones doing the hopping. Because there's not enough weight over the back wheels.

So my problem is bad brakes?

CLACK: No, no. The hopping is the problem, and the brakes don't cause that. I suggest you check your shock absorbers, which are there to damp the up-and-down action of your springs. They work just like the gizmo on a screen door that makes it close slowly. They're supposed to keep the wheels from hopping around.

CLICK: Know what else? Check your tire inflation.

Tire prices are going up?

CLICK: Hey, we're supposed to make the jokes. Some people tend to keep their tire pressure right at the upper limit, in an effort to maximize their mileage. That's great, but it takes away from the handling of the car, and also the braking.

CLACK: Makes sense; I mean, think about it. When tires are overinflated, less of the tire is touching the road, so when you step on the brake, it can have a tendency to break loose and hop a little.

CLICK: And it tends to wear out the middle of the tire.

CLACK: So try the same stretch of the road with softer tires. If that doesn't do it, check the shocks. Know how to do that?

Bounce on the bumper, right?

CLACK: Right, while a friend is driving the car at high speed on a smooth highway. . . .

CLICK: No, no, do it when the car is stopped. Get it going up and down and then jump off. If it keeps on rocking, you need new shocks.

CLICK: If it's rocking before you touch it, you need to quit drinking.

CLICK: If your shocks are more than three or four years old, you need shocks anyway. How old are your shocks?

Well, I've never had them changed. I bought the car in '86—

CLICK: Get new shocks. But check those tires too.

Less Than Round

Hi, my name is Heidi and I'm calling from Albany, New York. I have a question about tires. I recently bought an '88 Nissan Sentra, and the tires that came with the car are, well, less than round.

CLACK: Like square?

They're square. Almost square. Egg-shaped square. They bump, they make noise, and my mechanic said, "Get new tires."

CLICK: So he's right. Next question.

What kind of tires should I get? Several people have told me, don't get all-weather tires for a front-wheel-drive car.

CLACK: Don't get all-weather tires for any car. They're junk.

CLICK: They're a compromise for people who don't want to pay for snow tires, but need them. The cheapskates! I shouldn't call them that. I happen to have four of them on my own car.

CLACK: That proves that point!

Why are they so bad?

CLACK: Because you need a fine tread pattern for the rain, so the wheels won't "hydroplane," or scoot along on top of the water. You need a deep tread pattern for the snow. The in-between, which is supposed to do both, actually does neither very well.

CLICK: On the other hand, in the last couple of years computer-aided tire design has really improved all-weather radials, and the disparities are getting smaller.

CLACK: But I would recommend that you get real general purpose radials and then a set of snow tires too.

Tortured on the Rack and Pinion

CLICK: Hello, you're on the air.

I'm shopping for a new car and I want to know if I should get rack and pinion steering. What is it, anyway?

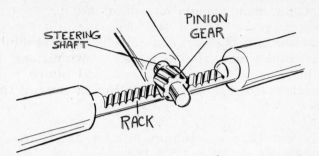

CLACK: Good question! Rack and pinion comes from the fourteenth century, during the Spanish Inquisition, when they put heretical automobile engineers on the rack and pinion to force them to recant.

CLICK: Rack and pinion steering is actually the most common kind of steering today. In fact, for the vast majority of new car buyers, it is the only kind of steering. It has supplanted, for the most part, the conventional steering-box setup that most cars had from the beginning of time. What it consists of is a pinion, which is a gear, and a rack, which is nothing more than a gear that has been opened up—a flat piece of metal with teeth on it. And they mesh.

CLACK: When you turn the steering wheel inside the car, the pinion turns and moves the entire rack gear to the left or right, which translates into moving tires left or right.

So what's new about it?

CLICK: It's not new. The widespread use of it these days comes from the popularity of front-wheel drive. With all that drivetrain gear in the front—engines, transmissions, axles, or whatever—there's no room for all the stuff that goes with the conventional steering box and linkage system they used to have.

CLACK: So if you don't want rack and pinion steering, buy a used car. And if you're buying a new car, you probably don't have any choice, unless you buy a full-size rear-wheel drive like a Caprice or a Crown Victoria. Don't let them convince you that rack and pinion is some special added feature. It's standard on most of today's cars.

The Cowboy Way

Hi. This is Sandy calling from Irving, Texas. One time you helped me and you were right on the nose, and now there's another problem.

CLACK: You expect us to be right twice? You're dreaming! But go ahead.

I have a 1981 Chevy Citation, and when it is cold—

CLICK: Don't tell me—you can't steer it.

You got it. I took it in and they replaced the power-steering pump—

CLACK: Oh, they were so close, but yet so far!

CLICK: I'd say they were about eleven inches away.

And $200 later, you know, it still does it.

CLICK: Of course, because the pumps almost never go. What goes is the rack and pinion steering assembly.

The what?

CLICK: The rack and pinion. It's better than the older system, when it works. But the truth is, General Motors came up with a crummy system on these earlier models.

There has been a problem with many GM cars. They don't steer when they're cold.

That's right! When the car's been left standing a few hours and the temperature's below 45, it takes all my strength to turn the wheel to the left.

CLACK: That's why General Motors has been promoting the "right turn only" law, so that no one will have to take left turns.

CLICK: You should get General Motors to kick in something for this. Some dealers will try to play stupid and tell you you have to pay, but don't do it. As of now, for cars that are less than five years old or have less than 50,000 miles, GM has decided to fix the problem free of charge. This is one of those cases when you'd have been better off going to the dealer in the first place, even though the car was out of warranty.

They would've fixed it correctly?

CLACK: Maybe. Depending on the dealer.

CLICK: Also, whoever put in that new pump should take it out, free of charge.

Yeah?

CLICK: Yeah. That's the cowboy way.

Welcome to *Car Talk*

CLACK: Hi, how are you?

You're supposed to say, welcome to Car Talk.

CLACK: Welcome to *Car Talk*, then, dammit.

Hello. I'm calling because I have an '82 Rabbit and I have to get new shocks for the front—I guess they're called McPherson struts—and I called a couple of local places and they said it'd be around $250. I also called a discount chain place and they said it would be $129. So I don't get it. They're all the same, right? They said they were McPherson struts.

CLACK: That's the type, not the brand. All these front-wheel-drive cars, and even some rear-wheel-drive cars, have McPherson strut–type suspension. Now, let's call them what they really are, they're just shock absorbers.

Like Monroes or Gabriels.

CLICK: More or less. McPherson is the name of the inventor. It's not a brand name.

CLACK: You can buy Kilimanjaro-brand McPherson struts, or you can buy El Gunjos. Just because the guy says they are bona fide McPherson struts doesn't mean anything.

CLICK: It's just a superbig shock absorber. It takes the place of some of the other suspension parts. Like the upper control arm.

So how do I know which ones to get?

CLICK: Good question. Either the $129 ones are junk, or the $250 guys are ripping you off, or maybe a little bit of both.

CLICK: But what she wants to know is, which of these two prices is the more reasonable one?

CLICK: Neither. $250's too high, and $129 is too low.

What should it be?

CLICK: We get like $175. That doesn't mean that that's the price you're gonna pay. But that's what we think the job should be worth, for parts and labor.

CLACK: People have this mistaken notion that all car parts are interchangeable, and that isn't true. Just like if you went out and bought yourself a suit—you know that you could buy a very expensive suit and a real inexpensive suit, and they would both be called a suit and be the same size, but they're not equivalent.

Right.

CLICK: It's the same with parts for your car.

CLACK: I disagree. I will give you the argument that the chains will use—that they depend on volume, and are buying the things a lot cheaper than Joe's corner gas station. They can give you a better price because they deal in volume.

CLICK: But they don't always give you the same quality that you would get, for example, by going to the dealer. I mean, I have bought exhaust systems from the chains and I have bought exhaust systems from dealers, and I know I am not buying the same exhaust system. They're not the same. You get what you pay for.

CLACK: Right! You get what you pay for. John Arbuckle whispers that in my ear every time I drive down the street. I say, "Oh, this noisy exhaust system's driving me crazy!" John Arbuckle says, "You get what you pay for, you cheapskate." And I say, "Okay, I can live with it."

Do I need an alignment when they replace the struts?

CLICK: It would be wise to get an alignment.

CLACK: Go for it. Get the $129 struts. It's a great price.

CLICK: Nah! Go for the $250 ones. Don't listen to him. You should see the car he drives!

Can I get heavy-duty ones?

CLACK: Oh, you can get heavy duty, extra-heavy duty, superextra-heavy duty. Whatever name you want on them, they'll stamp it on the box.

Can they make the ride better?

CLICK: They'll make it worse if you go too heavy duty. Seriously.

CLACK: You're not driving a dump truck here; this is just a little Rabbit. You don't need heavy duty; this car is too little.

Okay, thanks.

CLICK: Good luck.

Doing the McPherson Strut

CLICK: Hello, welcome to *Car Talk*.

Hi! My name is Janet and I'm calling from Des Moines, Iowa. I have an '86 Honda Accord, and it shimmies on the highway. I did everything. I even put new whaddayacallems on it. The struts, you know, the McPherson struts?

CLACK: Ah, yes, the McPherson strut. It's a new dance. We didn't know it had made it out to Iowa.

CLICK: What about your tires?

That's when it all started. They're new.

CLACK: Aha! The plot thickens. It didn't do this with the old tires?

No. According to my mechanic, the new tires made the problem show up.

CLICK: Sounds screwy to me. Your mechanic has it backward.

How could it be the tires? They're brand new.

CLACK: How much did you save on these tires? Did you get an especially fantastic deal?

Well, as a matter of fact—

CLACK: I thought so! They're cheap tires. Don't you remember Click and Clack Adage Number One! "It Is the Stingy Person Who Spends the Most!" So you've gone for all these balancings, and alignments, and struts, and now you have to buy four new tires anyway. Your cheapo tires are "out of round."

Out of round?

CLICK: We've seen many instances where we find tires, both foreign and domestic manufacture, that aren't round. Now, you may say, "Oh, my tires are round, they sure ain't square."

CLACK: But, in fact, they may not be round enough.

CLICK: It's like extra-virgin olive oil. There's round and then there's extra round.

Rrrrrrrrrrrrrrrrrrr

CLICK: You're on the air.

Hello. My name's Mary. I'm calling from Indiana.

CLICK: Hi, Mary. What's up?

I've got a 1980 Toyota Corolla. It's got about 125,000 miles on it. I had new tires put on it a year ago. They were new Michelins, and as soon as I got them on, I noticed this droning noise that was very pronounced.

CLACK: Make the noise for us, Mary.

It's kind of like Rrrrrrrrrrrrr. *It's medium-pitched.*

CLACK: It doesn't sound like a metallic sound, does it?

No. I took it back in and they said, "These are very hard tires. They're loud tires." I said, "Oh."

CLICK: Oh.

But when people ride in my car with me, they say, "What's that noise?"

CLACK: You didn't happen to buy all-weather tires?

Yes, I did.

CLACK: Oh! There's your mistake! All-weather tires are noisier.

CLICK: No, that's not a mistake. That's what you should have on the car.

They're the same kind of tires that came with the car, and I didn't notice it then. My cousin-in-law rode with me and he said, "Oh, Mary, it's your rotors. You've got something wrong with the rotors."

CLACK: No, your cousin's got something wrong with his rotors. He doesn't know what he's talking about. It's the tires. The original tires that were on there may not have been all-weather tires. Also, it's true that some tires may be harder and make more noise—

CLICK: As stupid as that sounds.

CLACK: But it's also possible that the noise you hear is not the tires at all. It may be just a coincidence that it started at the same time you got the new tires. This happens; people often underestimate the power of coincidence.

CLICK: Particularly mechanics, who like everything to be logical.

CLACK: For example, maybe a wheel bearing went bad. Now, these clowns at the tire store, they don't know about wheel bearings. All they know is tires. Mount them. Balance them. Stick them on the car, and collect your money. So when you go in there with a noise, they look at the tires, and if they're not square or flat on one side, they send you home.

CLICK: Are you speaking pejoratively of the tire dealers of America?

CLACK: I don't even speak Pejorative. Where is Pejora, anyway? Look, it's possible that this isn't a tire noise. Go to your regular mechanic. You have one, I trust.

Okay.

CLACK: Let him drive it. Any half-decent mechanic ought to be able to discriminate between a wheel-bearing noise and a tire noise. And if it is the tires, and he says it's an acceptable amount of noise, don't worry about it. They may get quieter as you drive the car and they wear in.

CLICK: Not likely. The drone will actually impair your hearing.

What?

Shocks

CLICK: Hello, welcome to *Car Talk*.

I've got an '85 Saab. My boyfriend thinks the shocks are in need of replacement. . . .

CLICK: Does he want to drive the car?

He already does.

CLACK: That's probably why they need to be replaced. It probably won't corner at 95 anymore, since he's worn out the shocks.

What are shocks for, anyway?

CLACK: You mean, what do they do? They slow down the movement of the springs, so the car won't keep bouncing up and down.

CLICK: So get them replaced. It's not too expensive.

These are gas shocks. Do I have to replace all four?

CLICK: No, you can replace them in pairs.

CLACK: Yeah, replace the two left ones if you usually turn to the right. Or the two right if you're more inclined to turn left. No, seriously, do front or back in pairs. Original-equipment shocks last, at best, a couple of years.

All right, thanks. I've got one last question. Which one of you guys is Click, and which one is Clack?

CLACK: That's easy. He's Click.

CLICK: And he's Clack.

Two Left Tires

CLICK: Good evening.

I have a question about some tires. I have a couple of used radial tires that I picked up cheap, and I don't know which one was on the right side and which one was on the left side. The question comes up, what effect will it have if I put them on the wrong way?

CLICK: Well, one of the things that sometimes happens is that the tire will come apart. It depends what kind of a history it has. If a tire is on a car on the left side for 50,000 miles and you put it on the right, there's a fair chance that it'll come apart.

How soon and how violently?

CLACK: You can assume that it'll come apart when you're going fast. And that often means violently.

CLICK: One way you can tell is by the amount of noise the tires make when driven on a road. For example, put the tires where you think they go, eenie meenie miney moe. . . .

One side or the other?

CLACK: Yeah, it doesn't make any difference, because you don't know where they belong anyway.

Right.

CLICK: Then drive 40 miles per hour on a quiet road and listen.

Okay.

CLICK: And then swap 'em and see if it's quieter.

Okay.

CLACK: Since it's only two tires, that shouldn't be too bad. Usually you can tell if you listen carefully—you can usually hear some kind of a difference.

That seems to make some sense.

CLICK: And if you can't tell, leave 'em on and drive it and wait for the worst to happen. Which may never happen.

And make sure I have a spare tire.

CLACK: Yes. And don't drive over a hundred.

They don't have much mileage on them. That's the reason I picked them up. They're a used pair and I'm not even sure that they were a pair, necessarily.

CLICK: Better that way. That way, at least only one of them might be wrong. Because if they were really a left and a right pair and you were wrong, you can't be wrong with one, you gotta be wrong with two.

CLACK: But you wouldn't necessarily be right with two, either. In fact, you might always be wrong with one, no matter what you do.

This is too confusing. Thanks so much.

CLICK: Any time . . .

The Rust Bucket

Hello. I drive a rust bucket.

CLICK: Good. I'll let my brother answer this question, then.

Okay. It's a 1977 Datsun B210. I bought it brand new for $3,000. About a year ago, before I moved back here from Florida, I was hearing this noise from the front end. Especially when I went over rough pavement.

CLACK: Uh-huh.

I brought it to a mechanic. He called me up later that day and said every piece in the front that can wear out—

CLACK: Had to be replaced.

—was worn out.

CLICK: Right.

And he said he could replace it all for a few hundred dollars—

CLACK: Five hundred, probably.

Yes, but he said that it wasn't worth it because he would just be attaching new pieces to rust.

CLACK: Amazing, an honest man.

Everything was rusted out, he said, including the frame itself. That was over a year ago, and since then I've driven the car up from Florida.

CLACK: What?

I still drive it around occasionally.

CLICK: You didn't do the front-end work?

No, he suggested I don't do it, and just look for another car.

CLACK: And you're driving this car today?

I drove it here from Florida, yeah. I even asked him, "Is it safe to drive?"

CLICK: I hope he didn't say yes!

CLACK: Did he have a mad chuckle? An insane, diabolical laugh?

Well, he said I should pay attention to the sound of the car, and once it started to sound funny—

CLACK: Did he send you to the sporting goods store to buy a football helmet?

No, he said pull it to the side of the road and never drive it again.

CLACK: Aha, you see!

CLICK: Look, you've got two problems. The rust problem of the frame is dangerous to the extent that if you should have a serious accident, the car will literally crumble and fall apart.

Uh-huh.

CLICK: But even more serious than that, if you need every single piece of the front end: tie rods, ball joints, idler arm—then any one of those things can break at any time. So if you're driving at 50 or 60 miles per hour, and one of them breaks, you're done for. I mean, the wheel falls off.

CLACK: Things get hairy when a wheel falls off.

Well, I don't drive it that much. But the other day when I was driving it, when I got it up to about 40, the steering wheel started shaking.

CLICK: Oh, my God.

CLACK: No, seriously, this is no joke, you are driving a death trap. Do not drive the thing anymore. Tomorrow morning, call Artie's junkyard. He'll give you five bucks for it, and it's the best five bucks you'll ever get, because it will save your life. Okay?

CLICK: He hung up. . . .

The Law of Diminishing Returns

Hello, is this Click and Clack?

CLICK: Who else? Who's this?

My name's Craig. I'm calling from Arlington, Texas, and I've got a 1986 Pontiac Firebird. Now, is that a mistake already? Why are you making that noise?

CLACK: We just groaned a little.

It's got a noise coming from the front, like in the wheels, and it started when the car had about 3,000 miles on it. It started going shoop, shoop, shoop, and after a little while I noticed that the left front tire started scalloping on the outside. So I rotated the tires and the noise went away. Then about 3,000 miles later, it started coming back.

CLICK: What do you mean, you rotated the tires?

You know, put the left front to right rear and vice versa.

CLICK: Okay. You first got the noise at 3,000 miles? Brand-new car?

Right. And now the noise is back.

CLACK: How many miles on the car now?

The car's got 22,000 miles on it, but the noise occurs every 3,000 miles. I just rotate the tires and it goes away for 3,000 miles.

CLICK: What's happening here is that your wheels are way out of alignment.

Well, now, that's another thing. I've got one of those lifetime alignment deals and I get it aligned every 5,000 miles.

CLICK: Oh, I'm sure they do it every time you go in, too!

CLACK: Right. They pull you in, they give you a cup of coffee, they drive your car out the back door, they sit in it and listen to the radio. They say, "Yeah, this alignment's great. Those speakers are lined right up!"

CLICK: They turn on the headlights and see if they both point toward the front and they say, "Great." No, this is a classic.

CLACK: When you rotate the tires, what you're doing is putting the bad tires on the back and the good tires on the front. The noise goes away for a while; meanwhile, the scalloping is getting worn off of the old front tires because they're on the back. They get doctored up a little bit. The noise comes back and what do you do? You rotate the tires again. Every time you do this it takes less time for it to get bad. Right?

I guess.

CLICK: You are invoking the law of diminishing returns. These guys who claim to be checking your alignment, aren't. Even though you have some kind of an alignment warranty, take it somewhere else. Go to the dealer and when he tells you the alignment is way off, go back to the first guys and sue them for four tires.

Okay.

CLACK: And an alignment. But don't have the alignment done by them. Seriously. Forget these guys.

The Guinness Book of World Records

Hi, my name's Chuck, calling from Warrensburg, Missouri. I have a Vista made by Mitsubishi.

CLACK: A Colt Vista.

Yeah. It's four and a half years old with 94,000 miles on it. It's in great shape except for the front end. When you drive about 60, the steering wheel shakes. I took it to my mechanic and he said that the front tires are cupping. I'd never heard of that before. He thinks that I should rotate them. But the back tires are the original tires. They're in good shape. I've never heard of cupping. Is that what it sounds like to you?

CLICK: Yes. Are these front tires also originals?

No. I replaced them about 30,000 miles ago.

CLACK: 30 or 40,000 miles is about all you can get out of tires on a front-wheel-drive car, unless you're really lucky.

Really? Then what causes cupping?

CLICK: Two things. Bad alignment and bad shock absorbers, which you probably have.

CLACK: 94,000 miles and you've never replaced the shocks, I'm sure.

No, I never was told I should.

CLICK: Well, that's the fault of your mechanic. You've been told now. If you have struts that still work after 94K, then you should write to the Guinness Book of World Records. When you have bad shock absorbers, you don't just get a bad ride. The tires bounce.

CLACK: They're bouncing, and every time they come off the road and then hit again, they get scuffed. That causes not only poor handling, but the cupping eventually.

But you can't see that on the tire though, right?

CLICK: You can feel it. If you run your fingers along the surface of the tire, you will feel it go up and down, like little waves. Every time it bounced and came down and hit the road, it wore away a little piece of the tire.

CLACK: When you're driving on wet roads and you're bouncing around a lot, your braking distance increases tremendously. Figure it: your wheels are off the road a third of the time, so how can they stop you? It's dangerous to drive around on bad shocks.

CLICK: So here's what you do, Chuck. You buy two new front McPherson struts, and four new tires. The ones in the back that you think are still good after 94K—toss them too.

Oh, come on. They look great.

CLACK: I don't care what they look like. Throw them away. Tires aren't made to go that long. The sidewalls are probably all cracked. They're ready to blow out and take you with them.

CLICK: They're cheap. You've got little old 13-inch wheels. You can probably get tires at Toys "R" Us.

So you're saying struts and what else?

CLACK: Four new tires. Struts, alignment, and then see how it drives. Shoot the moon. I mean, you haven't spent much money on this car, have you? Tell the truth.

No, I haven't spent much.

CLACK: It's been a wonderful car, hasn't it? So quit being such a cheapskate.

THE LAST WORD

You can see from our calls that the suspension and steering aren't things toward which you should take a cavalier attitude. Some dangers give you warnings and some don't. Any unusual handling or vibration *could* be a warning of dire events about to happen. Don't ignore them. If you do, you tend to get used to them. Others are even more insidious because they *don't* give you any warning! They require careful inspection by a pro. This is what state safety inspections are for. Take your car to a garage that will find things wrong with your car, not to the places that blow the horn and then slap on an inspection sticker.

The best example of a potentially dangerous "invisible" problem is ball joints. The ball joints hold the wheel to the rest of the car. In fact, they're the *only things* that hold the wheel to the rest of the car. They can wear out so that the driver (even a pro) won't know it. No noise and no vibration—and then you hit a bump in the road and the wheel ends up looking cross-eyed.

Have your ball joints checked once a year, at least! And specifically ask that they be checked. And watch them do it, if you can. (If he doesn't jack up the car, he didn't do it!)

Don't say, "I can live with it." You never know.

One final word: whether you go for regular maintenance or not, and even if you had your alignment done or you brought the car in four weeks ago and everything was pronounced A-okay, at the first sign of anything shaking or doing anything unusual, don't just assume that it's something that's going to go away, because nothing ever goes away. And don't just assume that it's something benign, because you never know. Most people, either out of inertia or unwillingness to take the time to take it to somebody to get it looked at, end up getting themselves in dangerous positions. So if there's something that the car does, especially if it's very sudden, get it checked. If it was behaving beautifully yesterday and it's shaking and shimmying and vibrating all over the place today, there's usually something very, very wrong. And again, it could be something simple like a tire that's out of whack or maybe your boyfriend or girlfriend drove into the curbstone with your right front wheel and didn't want to tell you. No matter what, if you notice a big change from one day to the next, then get it looked at right away, because the next ride could be your *last* ride. Or the next car ride you take could be in one of those long black jobs.

MORE POINTLESS NOSTALGIA

Remember in the old days, when you used to go in for a lube job? A lot of cars don't require lube jobs anymore because they don't have grease fittings and they don't have pieces that require periodic greasing. They use ball joints and tie-rod ends that are sealed, and they put rubber boots over them and you don't have to worry about them anymore.

Well, that creates a problem, because if no one's under there greasing the car, nobody's looking. Even when you get your oil changed, they don't notice that the boots are torn open or that, in fact, the tie-rod ends are all worn out. You're not going to check it because you don't know what to check.

But there's a way around this problem. Here's what you are going to do, once a year—now, promise—you're going to have the alignment checked.

You know, it's amazing. Years go by really fast. People say, "Oh, yeah, I had that done last year," and then when they check their records they find out it was four years ago. Especially as you get older, the years kind of all melt together and you don't really remember one year from the next year.

Believe me, we know about this.

One year turns into two, which turns into three or four, and the next thing you know, you have a car that's eight years old. But you just bought it two years ago, and you're wondering how this could happen.

So whether you have a light car or a heavy car, get that front end, get that suspension, get that steering mechanism, get all that stuff checked once a year, at least, by having your alignment done. That's the best way to be sure that everything is in good shape. And also, if you do it every year, you're not going to get those nasty surprises. People are always coming out of the shop with this shocked look on their face because they found out they needed $600 worth of new tires and front-end work, but it wouldn't have looked so bad spread out over four years.

BRAKES

If oil is the most important maintenance item in your car, in terms of saving you money in the long run, brakes are the single most important safety item. The brake system is actually the most important system on your car, period. If your engine doesn't work, the worst that can happen is you miss work, and have to call in sick. If your brakes don't work, and you find out when you are doing 65 on some superhighway, then somebody else will have to call in sick for you. And they won't be lying.

All of today's cars, with a few exceptions, like the Tibetan Yak Tracker, have disc brakes on at least two wheels. Usually it's the two front wheels, because these are the wheels that do most of the work in stopping.

Disc brakes are simple. Most of you are familiar with the mechanism on a bicycle, where you pull the lever and the device—it's called a caliper—squeezes the wheel and slows you down. Disc brakes on a car work exactly the same way. They are more complex and heavier, of course: instead of having a mechanical coupling—a cable that squeezes the caliper shut—they are hydraulic. This means that when you step on the brake, brake fluid is squeezed through lines (by the action of your foot) and pushes the caliper shut. But the principle is the same.

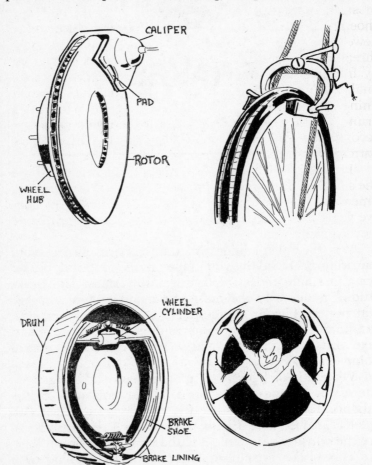

The brake caliper has two pads on it, which rub on a disc attached to the wheel, called the rotor, to slow you down.

Drum brakes, used mostly on rear wheels these days, have two shoes that press outward against the inside of a drum, accomplishing the same end. A hydraulic wheel cylinder pushes the shoes out.

Brake pads, found primarily on the front wheels, and brake shoes, which are found only on the rear wheels of most cars, are designed to wear out. A brake pad or a shoe has a lining made of asbestos in older cars, and in newer cars some soft metallic materials, which are not so threatening to our lungs. So as the brakes get worn away by friction, these linings get thinner and thinner until finally they're all gone. What's left is the steel that the lining was bonded to, rubbing directly on the rotor or the drum. When you get to that point, all of your stops are accompanied by a sound not unlike that of a ship's bottom being scraped clean by the Great Barrier Reef.

Pretty scary, isn't it? This is a good reason to get one's brakes looked at from time to time. From time to time means once a year if you have a newer car (less than five years old) and every six months if your buggy is, as they say, more mature.

When your car is in for this brake checkup, more than just the linings should get checked. So if you're bringing it to Fred and Millie's Filling Station and Dance Studio, and they're giving your brake system a quick exam by pulling off one wheel, that's not good enough. You might want to suggest that the other three wheels have brakes attached to them, too, and you'd like them *all* looked at.

When all four wheels have been removed, all kinds of interesting things can be seen. If the right-side brake pads are worn more than the left, a sticking caliper might be revealed. Rear wheel cylinders should be checked for leaks while the rear linings are checked for wear. And while the rear brake drums are off, the parking-brake mechanism can be checked to see if the cables and the levers are free. (Yes, the parking brake is a mechanical and not a hydraulic system.)

If you own a Saab or a Subaru, the parking brake is on the front wheels. Don't ask why. You don't really want to know.

And of course, lastly and most importantly, all of the brake lines—the stainless-steel tubing that carries the brake fluid from the master cylinder (which your foot pumps) to the individual wheels—should be checked for rust and leaks. Ditto for the flexible rubber lines that go to the front wheels (so they can move up and down and turn corners).

Only when all that is checked out can the dance class begin.

Most things in the brake system wear gradually. Discs (or rotors, as mechanics persist in calling them) warp gradually, master cylinders usually fail slowly, wheel cylinders begin to leak slowly. So how do you notice this stuff? You don't. But if you're going in for your checkup every six months and getting your linings looked at and your hydraulics looked at, these things will be noticed.

And don't be surprised when wheel cylinders leak and calipers seize and need to be replaced. Because all of this stuff has a life span that, on modern cars, seems to be getting shorter and shorter. I think one of the things that has happened over the past fifteen or twenty years is that manufacturers realized that they were making some of the components too good. They were lasting too long. So now they're making them not so good, which means you've got to check them a little bit more often.

It looks like there's a lot that can go wrong—and you know what? There is! But fortunately, all cars sold in America, including the much-feared Tibetan Yak Tracker, are required to have a dual braking system. (Thanks to the late AMC [American Motors], I think. They were the innovators of this system.) What this means is that half the system is separate or isolated from the other half, so that if half of it fails, you still have the other half.

Most companies separate the front and the rear wheels. If you lose the front brakes, you have the rear brakes, and vice versa. Or versa vice. There are some companies that really *thought* about it (like Volvo, Mercedes, Saab, and a few others), and separate them diagonally, which is the best way to do it, since rear brakes are only one third as effective as front brakes. But front to rear is better than nothing at all. In any event, we all agree that one third of a loaf is better than none, and we should give thanks to Uncle Sam for watching over us.

No brake check can be complete without a road test. So before Fred puts on his tutu for the next dance class, he should take your car for a spin. He'll be trying to find out if your buggy pulls left or right when braking or if the wheels lock up on a moderate to hard stop. He will also notice if the stopping distance is okay or not okay. A pulsing pedal could tell him that your discs or drums are warped and in need of machining or maybe even replacing.

All this can be found out in a very short test drive, and they are things you might not notice yourself. In fact, you are less likely to notice them because the changes are slow and usually subtle, and we all tend to compensate for Old Bessie's shortcomings. But Fred, if he's serious, will sniff out these problems when he takes your car for its road test.

You might think that this thorough brake check leaves you with nothing to do. No such luck. What you can do and should do is *listen* from time to time. That's right, listen. Turn off the radio, drive on a quiet street, and apply the brakes. If you don't sense the presence of that grinding Great Barrier Reef, that's great. It's okay for now, but you have to make sure you do this once a month. Sure you will.

Or you might hear another noise. Some cars have a little thing called a wear indicator on the brake pads. It's just a little piece of metal, a vibrating reed that makes an annoying noise when it comes into contact with the spinning disc rotor. When the pads are worn out, this little reed makes contact with the disc and sits up and sings.

This noise is meant to be very annoying, because it's telling you something is wrong. Don't ignore it. If you do, within a week or so, that reed that's been oscillating many hundreds of times per minute and causing this annoyance in your life will eventually fall off, and of course, that pain-in-the-neck noise goes with it.

Great! you think. Whatever was wrong fixed itself.

Wrong. The next noise you hear will be—you guessed it—the Great Barrier Reef Symphony.

Antilock braking systems are a relatively recent innovation. The reasoning behind antilock brakes is that you don't get your best stopping when your wheels lock up and your car begins to skid. The back end comes around to the front and you begin to spin, and that's usually not too good. So when you're stopping, you want all the wheels to be slowing down at the same rate. In other words, you don't want to lock up a wheel and have it skid.

Antilock braking systems (or ABS) became practical when computers entered the picture. The same kind of computers that make antilock brakes work will also help the IRS find you even if you move to East Treetrunk, Maine, and change your name to Hedley Lamar. You have to take the good with the bad, I guess.

Antilock brakes have sensors at each wheel, so if one of the wheels should begin to lock up, the antilock brake system interrupts the flow of hydraulic fluid to that wheel—in other words, reduces the brake pressure. It does this many times a second, so what the driver feels when slamming on the brakes on a wet or otherwise slick road, is that the pedal seems to be "crunchy" under his foot. It feels like someone is under there with a hammer tapping your foot. What you're feeling is the constant changing in the brake pressure—the antilock brake system at work.

And it really is phenomenal, take my word for it. I've driven many cars with ABS and really put them through their paces. Even on absolutely iced-over roads, when you hit that brake pedal, the car will stop almost perfectly straight, and in a shorter distance than it would ever stop with any kind of conventional brake system.

All cars these days have something called a brake warning light. This can tell you a few different things. One is that you've left the parking brake on and driven halfway to work. Whoops! Another is that there may be a leak or some imbalance of pressure in the hydraulic system. Or last but not least, the brake pads are worn out. When the light comes on, *get the brakes checked*. On older cars, which don't have a brake warning light, it's a good idea to find out where your brake fluid is and check it yourself from time to time. If you notice that you're adding fluid every three or four weeks, then get it looked at or buy extra medical insurance.

Under no circumstances, however, should you put black tape over the light. That's reserved strictly for oil pressure lights that won't go out. There'll be a special chapter on that in the next book.

There are other things we could talk about right now. Things like the importance of flushing out the hydraulic system periodically or the pros and cons of synthetic brake fluid, but we've gotta leave something for *Son of Car Talk*, right?

Don't ever buy a car, ever ever ever, without power brakes. Some of you older folks may balk at first. ("I had a '65 Catalina with power brakes, and every time I hit the brakes, my face wound up against the windshield and I had to keep buying new glasses and getting nose jobs.")

But forget all that. These days, power brakes are absolutely a requirement. Disc brakes, because they *don't* lock up like the old drum brakes sometimes did, require more pressure. Power brakes use the vacuum from the engine to assist in the braking, so you don't have to stand on the pedal to stop the car. It's a simple and foolproof system with hardly any moving parts.

So if you're looking at used cars (I don't think this is a problem with new cars, because they all have power brakes), be warned. Two older ones that come to mind are the Volkswagen Rabbit and the Chevy Chevette; they sold a lot of these without power brakes. You would step on the pedal and it felt great, except coming to a stop from 60 was very much a leg strengthening experience, and scary too.

So look for power brakes. Don't leave home without them.

Pads and Shoes

CLICK: Welcome to *Car Talk.*

My mechanic says my brake pads are about 40 percent gone, but he said they would last another year. This sounds crazy to me.

CLICK: No, he's not crazy. The pads work just as well when they are old as when they are new. He doesn't mean you have 40 percent braking power. You still have 100 percent.

CLACK: You're being negative; 40 percent gone means you have 60 percent still there.

CLICK: You should replace them when they're about 75 percent worn through.

What does "turn a rotor" mean? Do I have to pay for that every time?

CLACK: Well, if the disc rotors ever get scored or scratched by having the pads wear out, then they must get machined to make both of their surfaces flat and parallel again. Also, sometimes the rotors will get warped or will develop little ridges. And when you put on new pads, they don't mate to the rotors perfectly, and you will get shuddering or pulsing in the brake pedal when you step on the brakes. So it's not uncommon to have the discs machined at the same time that you put new pads in. It's tantamount to having a brand-new disc. Turning means to actually put them on a lathe and machine them. We have a lathe here for front-wheel-drive vehicles where we can actually machine the disc right on the car, which is terrific.

CLICK: You can sometimes get away without doing it, but most shops turn the rotors whenever they replace the brake pads. It's money well spent. Actually, on a lot of the smaller cars we just replace the rotors because they are so cheap.

The Horrible Burning Smell

CLICK: Hello, you're on the air.

My car! I was driving yesterday, and suddenly the whole front end was vibrating and the car was pulling to the left and after a time of this, I also smelled a burning smell.

CLACK: Stop, I know what it is.

You do?

CLACK: Yeah, yeah. But go ahead, we'll let you finish.

It cured itself.

CLICK: Right, as soon as you shut it off and let it cool off.

That's right.

CLACK: Yeah, and it's gonna happen again.

It is?

CLACK: I'm gonna take a guess as to what kind of car this is. It's a Chrysler Corporation car. A Valiant? A Volare? An Aspen?

You're right. A Dodge Aspen.

CLACK: What's wrong with your car is that you have a seized brake caliper. Your car has disc brakes in the front, and the things that squeeze the brake pads that actually slow down the wheel are called calipers. And one of them is seized, meaning that when you have taken your foot off the pedal, it thinks your foot is still on the pedal and it's still applying brake force to that one wheel. Left or right?

Right, I guess. The car wants to turn right.

CLACK: The other three wheels are free to turn. But that one wheel is stuck. Of course, the engine has enough power to still move the car, but it behaves very peculiarly.

CLICK: Don't drive, because it's very dangerous.

Is it really?

CLICK: Yeah. You could probably drive it to your service station if it's not very far from your house. But Monday morning get it to the shop.

And, uh . . .

CLACK: You want to know what it costs?

Yeah.

CLACK: It's not a whole lot of money. If you had a brake job done with both front wheels and a new caliper put on on one side, you'd probably spend less than two hundred bucks.

Why does this happen?

CLICK: Old age.

Old age of the brakes?

CLICK: Of the caliper. The caliper's probably the original one, it's never been replaced and the ones on the older cars go out after a few years.

I had a brake job done, within a year, anyway.

CLACK: How much did you spend for it?

About $150.

CLACK: For that price, they may have done front and back brakes. But my guess is, they probably didn't replace or rebuild any of the calipers. A year ago they could've been fine. In fact, a week ago someone could've looked at them and said, "Oh, these are fine." So it's not necessarily something that was overlooked by anyone.

CLICK: But that was then, and this is now.

Locked Brake

CLICK: Hello, you're on the air. You're on *Car Talk*.

Hi, there. My name's Clark, and I'm calling from Colorado. I'm calling about a friend's car, a 1982 Nissan Stanza,

which has had the emergency brake on for something like three months.

CLACK: And it's still on?

Right. We have tried everything. I tried to rock it back and forth, but I couldn't break it loose. Is this something I can fix myself?

CLICK: Well, yeah. There are a number of approaches. The emergency brake is a rear drum brake operated by a cable. What you need to do is get the car up in the air—

CLACK: What's he gonna do? Levitate it?

CLICK: No, you can jack up one rear wheel, then put something underneath the chassis, like the spare tire, so if the car falls off the jack, like they always do, it doesn't crush you. A safety stand would be better.

Okay.

CLICK: Then look for a cable going into the back of the wheel from the front of the car. Not the tubing; that's the hydraulic brake line. Look for a somewhat flexible cable housing. Shake it back and forth to break the rust, because that's what the problem is. The cable is rusted up in the housing and won't release the brake.

Should I pull the wheel off?

CLICK: You can't, for the same reason you can't turn it. The brake shoes are jammed tight against the inside of the drum. When you can turn the wheel it will mean you've succeeded. That's why you've got the wheel jacked up, to see if it will turn. Now, if shaking it doesn't work—

CLACK: And it won't, believe me.

CLICK: Cut the cable. Get a hacksaw or a big set of bolt cutters and cut through it, at which point you will have destroyed the cable, which is no good anyway, but you've released the tension on the brake.

CLACK: And then you can drive away.

Terrific.

CLICK: You can replace the cable later with a new one. You can drive without an emergency brake. They don't work in emergencies anyway. Which is why they don't call them emergency brakes anymore, I guess.

CLACK: They call them parking brakes, because when they freeze up on you, you're parked forever.

CLICK: But if you're lucky, you might be able to free it up by shaking the dickens out of it.

Okay, thanks.

CLICK: Good luck, Clark.

CLACK: You'll need it.

The Parking Place

CLICK: Hello, you're on *Car Talk*. Who are you?

I'm Linda, and I'm calling you about my beloved '77 Toyota Celica. It's never given me a moment's trouble until now.

CLACK: And you had to call us, huh?

Yeah. Anyway, this is my story. The brake light came on, you know, the warning light on the dash. I took it in and they said, "Gosh, your left front caliper is frozen open, and your master cylinder has got a slow leak." So I went to the local discount store and got a new master cylinder. They put it in. And when I took it out of the shop, it kept wanting to grind to a stop every time I took my foot off the gas. I took it right back and they said, "Okay, the pressure from the new master cylinder has forced your calipers closed, but now they're stuck closed instead of open." So they put on new calipers and turned the drums. They said, "Okay, it's driveable. Try it and bring it back in a few days. We want to change the rear brakes."

CLICK: How many CDs did you have to cash in to pay for this?

Actually, I haven't finished paying for it yet. They were going to wait till the very end before they bill me. Isn't that neat?

CLACK: Oh, yeah, they're going to have the paramedics there when you get the bill.

Maybe. Anyway, they said, "It's driveable." I take it about six blocks—they're really close to where I live—and I see this huge parking space right in front of my apartment! It's about two cars long, ideal; I'm coming up to it, and suddenly it's like I'm driving a riding mower down the street. I'm going like two feet per hour. Cars are passing me, you know, and they're giving me dirty looks.

CLICK: The brakes are stuck again?

Yeah.

CLACK: Did you get the parking place?

Yeah. I sort of oozed into it.

CLACK: So what's the problem? You've got it parked. Just don't drive it anymore. If you love the car, just go out and sit in it every day.

Well, here's the thing. I tried backing up, and the car wouldn't move. Okay. I shut it off. I come back about an hour and a half later, and I'm going back and forth in that big spot! Everything works again.

CLACK: And the buzzards are flying around!

No, not even that. So then I take it back to the shop again and the guy's looking really puzzled. So I say, "I'm gonna call Car Talk and tell them all about this." He said, "Go ahead."

CLICK: You came to the right folks, I'm telling you. You get the prize for the most interesting call we've had all day.

Well, that's nice for you. Not so hot for me.

CLACK: Well, what's even worse is that we don't know the answer.

CLICK: Yeah, we do, we do! In fact, we had this as a puzzler once on this very show.

CLACK: You're kidding.

CLICK: No, seriously, I know exactly what it is.

CLACK: So tell us, Mr. Holmes.

CLICK: Here's what's wrong. When you step on the brakes, the pressure in the master cylinder sends brake fluid through little tubes down to the wheels. Little metal tubes called brake lines. Except at the front of the car, it can't be metal tubing, because the wheels have to turn, right? So it's flexible tubing, rubber. Called flex hoses. Well, what happens sometimes is that this rubber hose collapses. If you have an old master cylinder, it's too weak to force the fluid through; you step on the brake and you get lousy stopping—

But I put a new master cylinder in.

CLICK: Exactly. Before you did, the caliper was stuck open, because there was not enough fluid coming through the collapsed hose to close it. So you put in a brand-new master cylinder; you get tremendous pressure, which forces itself through the hose, puts on the brakes—but now, since the hose is still collapsed, the pressure can't release! So the brakes are stuck on all the time!

But when I went back down . . .

CLICK: The fluid had slowly leaked back through and let the brake release.

CLACK: Brilliant! I love it!

CLICK: Here's how your mechanic can figure it out. He puts the car on the lift, and he has his assistant step on the brake. One or both of the front wheels will lock up. Probably just one. At that point, if he opens the bleeder, the wheel will unlock. That will let him know that the brake hose is plugged up and acting like a check valve.

CLACK: Use all these buzz words with him—bleeder, check valve, collapsed hose—maybe you'll get a job. But I bet you my brother's right. And this is the first time in decades.

CLICK: This is an easy fix. Don't worry about a thing.

"Eeeeeeeeeeeee!"

CLICK: Hello, you're on *Car Talk*.

This is David. I'm calling from Ringwood, New Jersey. I don't live here, though. I live in Akron. I'm visiting.

CLICK: Spare us the details. What's up, David?

Well, I've got a 1985 Honda Accord. It's got about 42,000 miles on it. And the wheels make a sound similar to the sound of the squeaking of the brakes. Except it does it whether I'm braking or not. It's a rhythmic sound. The speed of the sound is proportional to the rate I'm turning the wheels until I get—

CLICK: *"Eeeee!"* Is that it?

CLACK: You drive by the zoo a lot?

No, it's more high-pitched than that.

CLICK: *"Eeeeeeeeeee!"*

There, that's more like it.

CLICK: Well, here's what it is: On your brake pads you have a little reed of metal that's supposed to alert you that your pads are about to wear out. It's called a wear sensor. That reed of metal is hitting the disc and vibrating at a very high frequency and it's making this very unbearable noise.

CLACK: If you were a dolphin, you would hear it saying: "Replace Brake Pads, Replace Brake Pads." But you don't have the sensitive hearing of a dolphin, so you think it's just a squeak.

CLICK: Now what's going to happen is, if you ignore this squeak, the sensor will fall off and the noise'll go away.

CLACK: And you'll think everything's okay. And the next noise you hear will be: *Rgrgrgrgrgrgrgrgrgr.*

My wife's car already has *that noise! What is that?*

CLICK: That's the metal backing of the pads digging into your expensive disc rotors.

CLACK: The next sound you hear will be the rustling sound of hundreds of dollars leaving your wallet.

Is it dangerous?

CLICK: It's not undangerous.

CLACK: Of course it's dangerous. Every brake problem is dangerous.

CLICK: You can drive to the shop, if that's what you're wondering. But don't let it go unattended.

CLACK: It's better to travel in hope than arrive in disrepair, or something like that. Know what I mean? Get it checked out.

CLICK: Who said that?

CLACK: Lord Nelson. Thanks for your call, David.

Pump Up the Volume

CLICK: Hello, you're on *Car Talk*.

I'm Phil in Lexington, Kentucky. I have a 1986 Peugeot station wagon. It's a 505, and the brakes wear extremely fast.

CLACK: You probably drive extremely fast.

Well, we do put a lot of highway miles on it, but even so—I mean, the first set of pads lasted only 17,000 miles. And this set is going even faster.

CLACK: Who put on the second set? Was it the dealer?

Yeah. And it seems like they're wearing way too fast. The rotors seem to be okay, but the pads are going real quick, and there's always a lot of black powder on and around the tire and hubcap.

CLACK: Are they the same type pads? If you complained about brake squeaking, they might have gone to a softer pad.

Well, we did. They were very squeaky brakes.

CLICK: Aha!

I don't know if they went to softer pads or not, because they're still squeaky. Plus, we had the black powder before.

CLACK: The original-equipment pads on this car are a semimetallic composite. They're an amalgam of iron and brass and Clark's Teaberry Chewing Gum. But 17,000 miles is not terribly unusual for a set of pads. That's not too bad.

Well, on other cars I've had, I'd get 30 to 40,000 miles.

CLACK: Well, this is a Peugeot.

CLICK: We're talking about both front wheels, right?

Yes.

CLICK: Here's what you do. Have them machine the rotors and put on metallic pads, the original type. Don't worry about the noise. I had a similar problem with a Dodge Caravan that my wife drives, where I put on asbestos pads because the original metallic pads made too much noise. Except the asbestos pads made almost as much noise and they wore out to beat the band! So I threw everything away, and bought the original-equipment metallic pads and put them on. I told her to turn the radio up if she didn't like the noise. And it actually stops better. There's much less fade with the metallic pads. And you know what's funny? She turns the radio on loud whenever I get in the car.

CLACK: You got a good sound system?

Of course! It's great! Graphic equalizer. Six speakers.

CLACK: So, what are you worried about?

The Shuddering Van

Hi, this is Rosemary, calling from Newtonville, Massachusetts. I have a problem that is right up your alley, because it's very puzzling.

CLACK: Gee, you flatter us.

We have a 1985 Chevrolet Beauville van, which we just bought three months ago, used. We don't know anything about the history of the vehicle. It has 43,000 miles on it. After we'd had the van for about eight weeks, I encountered a problem. I was driving by myself when the van started shuddering, especially in the steering column.

CLICK: At what speed?

It was at about 45 miles per hour on a slight upgrade.

CLACK: And it had never done this before?

It had never done it before. Then I got my husband into the car, having described this to him—and for an entire month, including many drives purposely under the same conditions, it never happened again.

CLACK: And he doubted you?

He actually didn't doubt it too much. However, I was beginning to doubt it myself, because it never happened again. Then, a week ago, with three small children and all kinds of baby equipment, we got on the highway, and it started going crazy at about 45—the same thing, only worse. We couldn't even continue to drive it, because if nothing else it was shaking the van to bits.

CLICK: That was good judgment.

So we went to a tire dealer, because of course all this happened on a Saturday and this was the only place where there was any kind of mechanic. And they suggested that there might be too much play in the ball joints. So we returned home, because they couldn't fix it on the weekend. On Monday, we went to a bona fide Chevy dealer, who said, "Oh, you have a damaged wheel." And they replaced the wheel—the right front—realigned the front end, and rebalanced all the tires.

CLICK: Is there a happy ending to this story?

CLACK: Of course there's no happy ending! Think she'd be calling us if there was?

A happy ending? Yesterday the van did the same thing. As soon as we got above 45 miles per hour, it started shuddering again, only worse. Immediately and more dramatically.

CLACK: I could've guessed that. It's got to be something that's curing itself, and the thing that comes to mind—you said you feel the vibration in the steering wheel?

Yes, very much in the steering wheel.

CLICK: Good, good, good. What color is this van? Is it one of the earth tones?

It's a dull, metallic gray and red.

CLICK: Just as I thought! What I think is going on with your van, Rosemary, is that you have a stuck brake caliper.

Oh!

CLICK: An occasionally stuck brake caliper.

CLACK: I think I buy this too.

CLICK: Yeah. She's gonna buy one, too, I think! I don't like the ball-joint idea. I certainly don't like the wheel idea. That was bogus, if I ever heard a bogus idea. Did the guys at the dealership check your ball joints, in fact?

Yes, they did.

CLACK: Do these guys stand upright? Or do their knuckles scrape on the ground?

CLICK: No, no, they did their best. But I'd go for the occasionally seizing caliper, since it's an intermittent problem. What you have to do the next time this happens, which it certainly will, is get out and feel the front wheels, and see if one of them is much hotter than the other.

Touch the tire, the hubcap, or where?

CLICK: Touch the hubcap. One'll be much hotter than the other. Be careful, though. It might be hot enough to burn you.

CLACK: I presume, when they did the wheel balancing and alignment, that they checked all the front-end components. I always get nervous when it concerns steering. and make sure someone checks the universal joints. We didn't think U-joints until just now, but it's also a possibility. But the brake caliper is probably the best idea.

COOL IT!

When you make all those fires in the cylinders of the engine by burning gasoline, that engine gets really hot. So hot that if you just let it run, it would almost literally melt. So the engine has to be cooled before this happens. And since we're continually creating the heat, we have to continually remove it. This cooling is done by water—or a mixture of water and antifreeze if you don't live in Hawaii like we do. (Dream on!) Some cars used to try to cool the engine with circulating *air*. This was a bad idea and will always be a bad idea (even VW finally capitulated and now cools their engines with liquid). Here's how it's done.

First of all, the water has to come relatively close to the source of heat so that the heat can travel from the cylinders to the water. (We'll call it water, because it's easier to spell than antifreeze.) The engine is manufactured with small passageways all through it, and the water flows through these passageways.

So as the engine is running and heat is produced in the cylinders, the heat is transferred from the area around the cylinders to the water. This is good, but not good enough. Why? Because in a minute or so the water is hot enough to boil and that's the end of that idea.

Obviously, we can't let the water just sit there in the cooling passages. It would be nice to circulate the water. This is done with a *water pump*. It's really a very simple device—sort of like a bunch of little buckets stuck together in a circle.

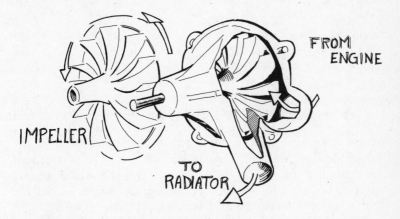

Camels turn these things in Egypt. You don't have a camel under the hood, but as we know from Chapter One (The Big Picture), spinning is one of the things that the engine is really good at. (Remember the spinning crankshaft?) Well, since the crankshaft is spinning anyway, it would be nice if we could use that spinning motion to turn the water pump. It turns out to be relatively easy to do this. Remember from Chapter One when we said that the crankshaft sticks out the back of the engine? Well, we can also let a piece of it stick out the front of the engine. If we put a pulley on it and another pulley on the water pump *and* connect the two pulleys with a belt, then the spinning motion of the crankshaft will be transmitted to the pump pulley and the pump will also spin.

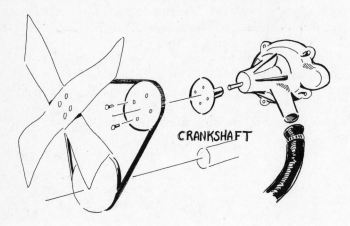

CRANKSHAFT

Now, whenever the engine is running, the water pump spins and the little buckets will throw the water from one side of the pump to the other; that is, the water will circulate. This is certainly an improvement over having the water just sit there. But it's still not good enough. Soon the water, circulating or not, will get too hot to cool the engine and we're back where we started: too much heat and nowhere to put it. We need to take the heat that's in the water and dump it somewhere. That's what the *radiator* does. If we add a radiator to the system and pump the water to the radiator, the radiator can— what? Right! *Radiate* the heat away.

The hot water is pumped into the top of the radiator and flows down long skinny flat tubes. As it travels down the tubes, the heat is transmitted from the very hot water

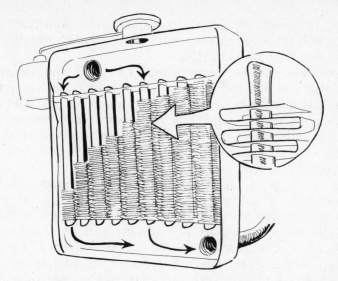

to the walls of the tubes. Now we have to get it away from the walls of the tubes, so we add little fins (they look like Christmas ribbon candy, the kind that really rots your teeth).

So the heat travels from the water to the tubes to the ribbon candy. Now what? Well, if we blow air across the radiator and the air goes through the fins, it will take the heat with it (and the heat will dissipate under the hood somewhere, which is not a real great place to dump it, but it seems to work).

Ram AIR

Where do we get the air? Well, if we're driving at 55 m.p.h., there's plenty of air flowing over the radiator, but at lower speeds, it would be nice to induce some flow— like with a fan. But what will power the fan?

You've got it! (You've been paying attention, haven't you!) If we could do that cute trick with the pulleys and belt to get the water pump to work, why not use it to get the fan to work too. And what have you got? Right! The ubiquitous *fan belt* (which, in most cases, is also the water pump belt).

Now, when the engine runs, the crankshaft turns and the belt makes the water pump pump and also makes the fan fan. Oh, this is brilliant!

Okay. Just a few more pieces and we'll have the entire cooling system. All of the pieces we've described so far are designed to make the engine run cooler. But we don't always want the engine to run cooler. Even though the engine shouldn't run too hot, it also shouldn't run too cool. When it's too cool, the gasoline won't vaporize correctly, and the engine stumbles.

So it would be nice to start this process of cooling things off *after* the engine gets up to the temperature at which it likes to operate. This is done by preventing the water from flowing to the radiator until the water temperature gets up to about 180 to 200 degrees. The device that prevents the water from flowing is the famous *thermostat*, which is just a temperature-sensitive valve that sits between the engine and the radiator.

It's a little valve closed by a spring. When you start up a cold engine, the crankshaft turns, the belt turns the

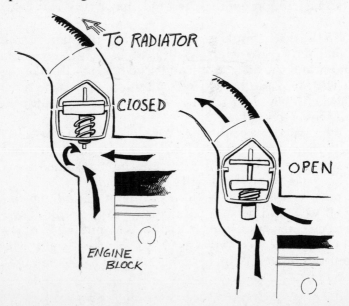

TO RADIATOR

CLOSED

OPEN

ENGINE BLOCK

water pump (and usually the fan) and the water starts circulating inside the engine. But when the water tries to get out of the engine to the radiator, it can't escape because the closed valve (the thermostat) is blocking the way. So the engine runs, the fires keep producing heat and the heat gets transmitted to the circulating (but captive) water, which keeps getting hotter and hotter. Pretty soon (five to fifteen minutes, depending on how cold it is where you live; here in Hawaii . . . but I digress) the heat from the water causes the thermostat to open. As it opens, it allows water to get to the radiator and everything begins to happen as described above.

The last piece of the cooling system is the heater. If it's cold where you live, it seems a shame to simply throw away all that heat when your tootsies are so cold. Especially since we're already pumping nice hot water around under the hood. So, we just add a couple of hoses and route some of the water to a smaller radiator under the dash, add another small fan (this time an electric one,

connected to a switch that says *fan* or *blower*), since you probably don't *always* want heat, unless, of course, you live up there in dog-sled country.

It works just like the radiator under the hood, except that instead of the fan and radiator dumping the heat under the hood, they dump it right on your cold feet.

Now you know how it all works. Isn't it great? I mean it really is pretty clever, isn't it? There are a few minor variations to the basic cooling system described here, but nothing really dramatic. Maybe the only one really worth mentioning is that some modern cars have an electric fan to blow air across the radiator, instead of a fan that runs by the fan belt/pulley arrangement. This electric fan operates only when the water temperature gets high enough to warrant it. You'll know if you have one of these because it almost always will come on when you're sitting in traffic. (When the car is moving it almost never runs). Sometimes it also runs *after* you shut off the engine. If you've wondered what that occasional whirring sound is, now you know.

Overheating

Hi, guys. Listen, I've got a 1965 Dodge Dart and it runs beautifully. It's got 86,000 miles and it purrs like a pussycat, and when I change the oil, wherever I go, the mechanic says, "Hey, you want to sell this car?"

CLICK: Yeah. This is what everyone should own: a car that the guy at the gas station tries to buy from you.

I don't want to sell it. My only problem is that if I hit traffic, and it's very slow, the needle begins to go pretty far up toward hot. I get nervous.

CLACK: Is the radiator as old as the car?

Sure! Everything's as old as the car!

CLICK: Except the driver. Are you as old as the car?

I'm older than the car!

CLICK: Is the temperature going up after you've driven it fast, and then you slow down?

Doesn't matter whether I'm going fast or slow.

CLACK: Oh, it's got to. I bet it cools off the faster you drive, right?

Right, once I start going, it cools off.

CLICK: I don't think this car had a 'fan clutch'. If it did, that would be the first thing I would suggest.

Is there anything I can do when it's happening? When it's heating up? Should I turn it off?

CLICK: No, it may not start again. Take it out of drive, put it in neutral while you're waiting, and keep it running a little faster than idle, you know, a sort of a fast idle.

CLACK: And turn the heater on full blast.

Are you serious? I'll die!

CLACK: Roll the windows down. Better you should die than the engine.

CLICK: But these are stopgaps. You may need a radiator flush. One of the things you should do if you really want to keep this car is to start flushing out the cooling system every ten to twelve years. I mean, you probably haven't done that, right?

Well, I go in and I say, "Give me antifreeze."

CLICK: Look. You mix water and iron engines together and what do you get? Rust. Even though all antifreezes have rust inhibitors' in them, they're only *inhibitors*. Sooner or later, you end up getting rust in here. *Not prohibitors*

CLACK: Little flakes of rust. But they look huge to the little tubes inside the radiator.

CLICK: What's going to happen, in the long run, is that all the cooling passages in the motor are gonna get plugged up. And then you'll really be in trouble!

So I get it all flushed out. How long can this buggy go?

CLACK: Forever! But every year or so you should have the cooling system flushed out. It's not just for the sake of the radiator. You can have someone take your radiator apart and clean the tubes. They actually stick 'rods down into the tubes and clean them out. Or, if worse comes to worst, you can throw the radiator away and buy a new one. But what about the passages *inside your engine block*? They're not so easy to get at.

CLICK: Or what about your heater core? It gets plugged up too. It only costs $50, but it's another $50 to $75 in labor to replace, since it's stuck up there under the dashboard.

CLACK: The only time most of us do something to the car is if something breaks. Well, by the time this happens, it's too late to do anything. It's like eating French pastry all your life, and then your doctor says, now you have arteriosclerosis. It's too late then to stop eating it, because the damage is done.

You guys are depressing me. I always put in 'permanent' antifreeze.

CLICK: On all these containers it says "permanent antifreeze." Do you know what that means? It means that it will permanently be antifreeze. It will never turn into a meatball, it will never turn into champagne, it will always be antifreeze. But that doesn't mean you can leave it in there permanently. You gotta get rid of the rust. You gotta flush the antifreeze out and throw it away so that you can get rid of the *rust that's in the system.*

CLACK: Here's a funny story. We once got a call from a guy who told us it was a terrible waste to throw away all that perfectly good permanent antifreeze just because it had rust flakes in it. So we said, "Yeah, but how do you get rid of the rust otherwise?" He said, "Easy! I've experimented for twenty years and the best way to purify old antifreeze is to pour it through a loaf of Wonder Bread. It works great! The antifreeze goes right through and the bread captures all the rust."

CLICK: I guess he's right, but I'll never eat a sandwich at his house.

Road Call

CLACK: Hello, you're on *Car Talk.*

My car's on fire.

CLICK: What?

I'm serious. I'm calling live, I'm at the side of the road at a phone and my car's on fire. What should I do?

CLACK: Calm down. Do you see flames or smoke or what?

Smoke. Coming from the front, up under the hood.

CLICK: Okay. Is it really smoke, or could it be steam? Hello?

CLACK: I guess she's gone to smell it. If it's really smoke, we should tell her to run, because it's too late. Why did she call us and not the fire department, anyway?

CLICK: The fire department doesn't fix cars.

Hello! It's steam, it's not smoke. It's hissing like crazy, but it's steam.

CLICK: Great. Now relax, and tell us what happened.

Well, isn't this crazy? I was driving along listening to your show and I saw this smoke—steam—and so I pulled over and called. I guess I was lucky to be put right through. I looked at the dashboard and the car was overheating, so—

CLACK: Whoa. First things first. What kind of car is it?

It's a 1984 Dodge Aries.

CLICK: Is it still running?

I shut it off when I saw it smoking. Steaming. It's steaming a little less now.

CLACK: You're just overheating. It means you've probably got a leak somewhere. What you want to do now is figure out how to get to a gas station without calling a tow truck, right?

Right, I guess.

CLACK: How far are you from town?

Oh, I'm right at the edge of town. I'm calling from Danbury, Connecticut. I know there's a gas station about two miles from here.

CLICK: Do you have access to any water?

There's a guy across the road watering his lawn.

CLICK: You're in luck. Wait till it stops steaming, then open the hood. Now, you have to wait a good half hour before it'll be safe to take off the radiator cap. Call us back then—in the meantime, find some rags you can use like a potholder.

Thirty Minutes Later: (She really did call back)

Okay. Now it's just sitting there. No more hissing.

CLICK: Great! Now use the potholder—the rags—and slowly unscrew the cap. If it's still hissing, stop.

No, it's not hissing.

CLACK: Good. Take the cap all the way off.

Now put the water in? The guy with the hose is here to help me out.

CLICK: No, don't put it in yet. If you put cold water in a hot engine you might crack something. Start the engine up first and add the water very slowly while it's running.

CLACK: I can hear it over the phone. Hear that clattering? She has a bad water pump. That's what let all the water leak out.

He's running. I always call my car "he."

CLICK: Okay, so now fill it to the top. When it's filled it might burp and belch a little, but it'll fill(Put the cap on, but don't tighten it, and scoot off to the gas station.

CLACK: No farther!

I'm gone. Thanks a lot.

CLICK: That's the first actual road service we've done over the phone.

Huh?

CLICK: Hello, you're on NPR's *Car Talk.*

Hi. My name is Mary Kay, from Syracuse, New York.

CLACK: Are you in the cosmetics business? Do you drive a pink Cadillac?

No. I have an '87 Chevy Cavalier. And I love my Chevy Cavalier, except I have one major problem.(I can't keep fluid in the reservoir.)

CLICK: Which reservoir?

The radiator. I had my radiator flushed out, and a week later I went back to check the temperature and there was no coolant in the reservoir. You know, the little plastic overflow one. The dealer checked for leaks, and he filled it up for me. And a week later it was gone again.

CLICK: How much did it take to fill it up? Were you there? Like a gallon?

CLACK: This is an important question.

It took probably a gallon.

CLICK: And how far had you driven it?

Well, it was a week. I guess about a hundred miles(But this has gone on for a year and a half)

CLICK: A year and a half! And you're adding coolant all the time?

Well, not all the time. I would add some and it would go along pretty good for three or four months, and then it would go again. And it's happening more often now. And I'll tell you what they did.[They replaced the thermostat, they checked the thermostat gasket, they replaced the lower radiator hose, they tightened the upper radiator hose and clamp . . .]

CLACK: Sounds like 'guessing' to me. If there's a leak, there's a leak. And they should be able to find out where the leak is.

I know. It's driving me crazy. They pressure test it every time I bring it in.

CLACK: This is the dealer? Take it to Mort's gas station. You know where Mort's is?

No.

CLACK: I don't either, but those turkeys at the dealer's have no interest whatsoever in fixing your car. You know what they want you to do?

CLICK: They want you to buy a new car, Mary Kay.

No, I'm not going to buy a new one. This car is good.

CLICK: Right, but do they care? Take it to some local gas station that's interested in your business. These guys don't want to fix it. I mean, if something is leaking, it's leaking. It's obvious. They put a pressure tester on it, they watch the thing for twenty minutes, and there's the leak. You gotta be a real ding-a-ling to misdiagnose a leak(Sometimes, for small leaks, you have to wait hours, though.)

CLACK: If they are checking it correctly and they can't find the leak, it's possible that there is no *external* leak.

CLICK: Right. The 'cylinder head' may be cracked, for example.

CLACK: Every time you go in there, they say, "Oh, yeah, no problem. We got it fixed now." And they charge you a nominal fee and put in a couple of cans of Stop-Leak. And you probably have more Stop-Leak than coolant in there.

No, they say they haven't put in any Stop-Leak.

CLACK: How do you know? Are you kidding me? They've probably poured in gallons of it. Plus mashed bananas. Plus oatmeal. Do you ever find empty Quaker Oats boxes in your trunk?

No.

CLICK: Seriously, it sounds like the leak may not be external, which means it's not a hose and it's not the thermostat gasket It could be leaking into the cylinder, vaporizing and blowing out the exhaust. This is not a leak that they can see. And if they haven't figured that out by now, they're clearly not going to. Go somewhere else, Mary Kay.

Well, okay.

CLACK: Get another opinion. And tell the new guys the whole sad story. Tell them that the dealer checked this and changed that, and then they'll figure out immediately that you've got an internal leak. It's either a cracked head or it's a bad head gasket.

Well, he checked the head gasket. He said that on the head gasket he found no yellowish residue, so—

CLICK: Oh, he doesn't know how to test it. Go to someone who knows how to do it. There are two tests that are done for the head gasket. When you go to your new shop, wherever that may be, ask him if he's gonna do both tests. If he looks at you and says, "Huh?" you say, "Thanks a lot, I'll be back tomorrow," and go someplace else.

The Ding-a-Ling

Hello, this is Lorraine from Belmont, Massachusetts.

CLICK: What's up, Lorraine?

I have a problem. I went to a gas station yesterday, and while I was getting gas, I said to the attendant, "I would like to buy something to put into my gas tank to make sure the gasoline doesn't freeze." He said, "Fine." So I followed him into the station—

CLACK: And he pulled out a pint of Jim Beam. . . .

Worse than that! He said, "Here, buy this," and it was a gallon of something. And I said, "I always buy it in little pints." And he said, "No, we only sell it this way."

CLICK: A gallon?

Yeah.

CLICK: What did it say on it?

It said, "ShellZone Antifreeze/Antiboil." Okay, so I took it. I said, "How do you measure this?"

CLACK: How old was this fourth grader?

He was at least six-four, probably a high school kid, and he was definitely not interested in selling me whatever I wanted—

CLICK: He sold you a gallon of antifreeze.

I know that now. But—

CLACK: Omigod. He didn't put it in your gas tank?

Well, listen to this. I asked him, I said, "How am I going to measure this and put it into my gas tank?" He said, "Pour it in till it spills over."

CLICK: Omigod.

I said, "Well, I only want a cup in, do you have a cup?" And he said, "No." So in front of him, I open up my gas tank and I pour the antifreeze into my gas tank, about a cup of it, and then I shut it and I leave. I take the thing home with me and I take it inside and I read it and I go—

CLICK: "Omigod."

Right. I go, "Omigod! This is for the radiator!"

CLACK: The moment of truth.

So I call my girlfriend and she takes me back to the gas station, and this kid says, "No, no, no, you told me, 'I want something for my radiator.' "

CLICK: Didn't he just witness you pouring it into the gas tank?

He watched me do it. Now, my question is, do I have to have my tank pumped?

CLACK: You have to have your stomach pumped!

CLICK: No, the truth of the matter is, if it was just a cup or so, it'll go right through the system—just like three chili dogs!

CLACK: What kind of car do you have, Lorraine?

Ford Escort, 1986.

CLICK: You won't even know the difference. At some point the car might hesitate a couple of times, but one cup out of the whole gas tank, you're probably not even gonna notice it.

I won't notice it? You're sure?

CLICK: Yeah. You might want to throw in a can of the stuff you really wanted, which is gas-line antifreeze.

Live It Up

CLICK: Hello, you're on *Car Talk*.

Hello, this is Bertha calling from L.A.

CLACK: Hi, Bertha. What's up?

I have a 1979 Plymouth Volare station wagon. I had the cooling system cleaned and they put in two gallons of coolant. When my recovery bottle gets low, shall I add straight coolant or half water?

CLICK: The level should not go down. I mean, it hasn't gone down already, has it?

No, it hasn't. I had it done about two weeks ago. We've had a lot of hot weather in L.A.

CLICK: That's why the coolant recovery bottle is there. When the car boils over, that coolant goes into this bottle. And when it cools off, the resulting partial vacuum will suck it back into the cooling system. Supposedly.

But when the coolant bottle gets low, I just wondered if I should add straight antifreeze.

CLICK: What you should add, theoretically, is a 50-50 mixture of antifreeze and water. But since it's not gonna be all that much, what you could do is put antifreeze in one time and water in the next time.

CLACK: Add a cup of antifreeze and pour a cup of water on top of it, and drink the third cup of water, and you're all set. Don't drink the antifreeze.

Can I even add above the limit line?

CLACK: Sure, why not? Live it up. The excess will just spill out onto the street and run down one of those earthquake cracks.

CLICK: The truth is, in L.A. you could just add water. In Los Angeles, you need antifreeze not because it freezes at a lower temperature than water, but because the 50-50 mixture will not boil over as readily as pure water in hot weather.

I have one more question. I have an unopened gallon jug of antifreeze. It's six years old. And I've been tempted to put it in, but I hesitate.

CLACK: Bertha, I've been waiting for this question for six years!

You think I can just put it in there?

CLACK: The answer is yes, you can do it because it says on the bottle "Permanent Antifreeze." In fact, some people say that antifreeze improves with age.

CLICK: Like auto mechanics.

Weep No More, My Baby

Hello, this is Rich. I'm calling from Normal, Illinois.

CLICK: Well, let's see how abnormal you are, Rich.

231 3800

I have a 1988 Oldsmobile Delta 88 and I'm leaking some radiator fluid. But the radiator and all the hoses are new. It's not leaking from any of the hoses or the radiator. It looks like it's coming right out of the front of the engine.

CLACK: Ah! You know what it's leaking from?

No, I don't. That's why I called you.

CLACK: For our Spanish-speaking audience, it is *la bomba de agua*—the water pump.

The water pump?

CLACK: Yes. Get a small mirror and a flashlight and put the mirror behind the top pulley at the center of the engine.

CLICK: The engine should be shut off when you do this! Run it till it gets warmed up, then shut it off.

CLACK: Shine the flashlight onto the mirror—you're going to look for a thing called a weephole. That's a small hole in the body of the pump where the water comes out when the seal is gone.

CLICK: Go and buy a new pump, unless—is this a good car?

Oh, yeah, it's a great car.

CLICK: Okay. Buy a new pump, because (many of the rebuilts are not very good.) You're gonna save a fortune putting it on yourself, so spend the money and do it right.

5

INSIDE THE ENGINE

The most expensive, if not the most dangerous, sounds a car can make are engine noises. They are also the least understood. This is because most people don't know what's inside the engine. They don't want to know. Most books either don't tell you what's in there, or they tell you in technical language nobody can understand. So we're going to break with tradition and tell you exactly what's in there.

Ready?

What's in there is a lot of expensive stuff.

To be more precise, what's in there are a lot of little parts that are hard to get at, so that when they have to be replaced, the labor will kill you. The biggest consideration when you have engine work done is the labor in getting the engine out of the car, getting it all apart, finding the one little part that went haywire, putting it all back together, and then trying to figure out what to do with the parts that are left over. That's the killer.

The parts themselves are really not that expensive,

it's just that there are so many of them and they all can break or wear out. Just to *list* them is labor intensive: in addition to the block and the cylinder heads there are the crankshaft, connecting rods, pistons, wrist pins, timing chain, timing belt (or suspenders if your engine is old-fashioned), connecting-rod bearings, camshafts and camshaft bearings, valves and valve-guide seals and valve springs. . . .

And while we're on the subject of valves, some engines now have four valves per cylinder. (The old standard is two.) One of the Japanese companies is even coming out with a five-valve-per-cylinder engine. Imagine that, a four-cylinder engine with 20 valves. Jeez! The machine shops are going to love doing valve jobs on these. You could buy a whole new car for what it's going to cost to grind the valves on one of these babies.

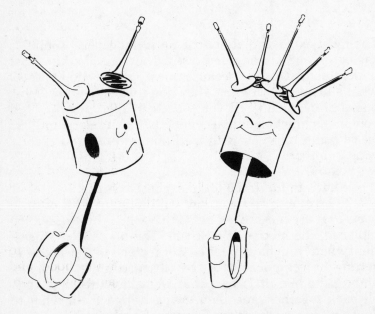

Anyway, to continue, there are hydraulic lifters, rocker arms, push rods (in some cases), oil pump, oil seals, front and rear seals and assorted gaskets, not to mention all the little pieces, like oil-pressure relief valves, which we won't mention.

So I won't mention them. Forget I mentioned them.

Anyway, you get the idea. So what can go wrong? With that much stuff in a small space, almost anything can go wrong, but most engine failure stems from neglect. And by that we mean either neglecting warning signals or neglecting the maintenance.

The engine's biggest enemies are (1) running too hot and (2) running too dirty.

A customer of ours had an old Thunderbird that he used to drive back and forth to New York to see a girlfriend every other weekend. And every time he made the trip he'd be in the shop the following Monday needing to get something fixed because the car was such a hopeless piece of trash. One Monday he failed to show up and Tom said, "Gee, that's kind of unusual." I said jokingly, "Maybe he blew the car up."

Well, what happened was that he was on the Merritt Parkway in Connecticut when he noticed that he had to keep the gas pedal all the way to the floor just to go 30 m.p.h., with this big V-8 engine, and he figured something was awry.

So he pulled into one of those filling stations where they sell gasoline and chocolate-chip cookies and milk. And he asked the attendant to look at the engine and, of course, the guy said, "I can't help you. All I know is cookies and milk." But the guy agreed to look anyway since our friend was really desperate. His girlfriend was waiting for him and he needed to know if he was going to make it. Anyway, the guy threw open the hood and jumped back in terror. The engine was glowing red. Somewhere along the line, probably around Hartford, he must have lost all of his motor oil. The engine kept getting hotter and hotter, but like a lot of other things in the car that didn't work, neither did his oil pressure warning light. As a result, the engine got so heated up that it fused itself together. All the pistons melted, and the cylinder heads deformed, and the pistons fused to the cylinder walls, and the bearings welded themselves to the crank- shaft—oh, it was a terrible sight! When he tried to restart the engine, he just heard a *click, click, click* since the whole thing was seized up tighter than a drum.

That's what can happen in a case of extreme engine neglect. Most of us wouldn't do that, or at least wouldn't do it knowingly. Our friend didn't do it knowingly either, but he learned a valuable lesson. He learned that his girlfriend wouldn't come and get him if his car broke down. Even if he offered her cookies and milk.

The oil is critical to keeping things running since it not only acts as a lubricant, but it also helps to keep the engine cool. What happens is that the oil pump sucks the oil out of what's called the sump (or the crankcase or the oil pan), and it pushes that oil, under pressure, up to all of the parts that need lubrication.

The way the oil works is that it acts as a cushion. The molecules of oil actually separate the moving metal parts from one another so that they don't directly touch; the crankshaft *journals*, or the hard parts of the crankshaft, never touch the soft connecting-rod *bearings* because there's a film of oil between them, forced in there under pressure. From the pump.

It's pretty high pressure too. When the engine is running at highway speed, the oil, at 50 or 60 pounds or more per square inch (or about 4 bars, if you're of the metric persuasion—but let's leave religion out of this), is coursing through the veins of the engine and keeping all these parts at safe, albeit microscopic, distances from each other.

But if there's a lot of dirt in the oil, the dirt particles get embedded in these metal surfaces and gradually the dirt acts as an abrasive and wears away these metal surfaces. And pretty soon the engine is junk.

It's also important that the motor oil be present in sufficient quantity. In nontechnical terms, that means there's got to be enough of it in there. If you have too little oil in your engine, there's not going to be enough of it to go around, and it will get very hot, because four quarts will be doing the work of five, and so forth. When that happens, the oil gets overheated and begins to burn up at a greater than normal rate. Pretty soon, instead of having four quarts, you have three and a half quarts, then three quarts doing the work of five. And then, next thing you know, you're down to two quarts and your engine is glowing red, just like that guy driving to New York, and it's chocolate-chip cookie time.

In order to avoid this, some cars have gauges and some have warning lights; some people call them "idiot lights." Actually, we prefer to reverse it and call them "idiot gauges." I think gauges are bad. When you drive a car—maybe I'm weird about this—I think it's a good idea to look at the road most of the time. And you can't look at the road if you're busy looking at a bunch of gauges. It's the same objection we have to these stupid radios today that have so damn many buttons and slides and digital scanners and so forth that you need a copilot to change stations. Remember when you just turned a knob?

Not that gauges are bad in and of themselves. I think if you have your choice, what you want is idiot lights—or what we call "genius lights"—and gauges too. It's nice to have a gauge that you can kind of keep an eye on for an overview of what's going on. For example, if you know that your engine typically runs at 215 degrees and on this particular day, which is not abnormally hot, it's running at 220 or 225, you might suspect that something is wrong and get it looked at before your radiator boils over.

On the other hand, if that gauge was the only thing you had to rely on and you didn't have a light to alert you when something was going wrong, then you'd look at the thing all the time, especially if your engine had melted on you once. In that case, why don't you take the bus? Because you're not going to be a very good driver, spending most of your time looking at the gauges.

Incidentally, if that oil warning light ever comes on, shut the engine off! We don't mean that you should shut it off in rush-hour traffic when you're in the passing lane. Use all necessary caution and get the thing over to the breakdown lane. But don't think you can limp to the next exit, because you can't. Spend the money to get towed and you may save the engine.

It's a little-known fact that the oil light does *not* signify whether or not you have oil in the engine. The oil warning light is really monitoring the oil *pressure*. Of course, if you have no oil, you'll have no oil pressure, so the light will be on. But it's also possible to have plenty of oil and an oil pump that's not working for one reason or another. In this event, a new pump would fix the problem, but if you were to drive the car (saying, "It must be a bad light, I just checked the oil!") you'd melt the motor.

So if the oil warning light comes on, even if you just had an oil change and the oil is right up to the full mark on the dipstick and is nice and clean—don't drive the car!

Here's another piece of useful info. When you turn the key to the "on" position, all the little warning lights *should light up*: the temperature light, the oil light, whatever other lights you may have. Because that is the *test mode* for these lights. If those lights *don't* light up when you turn the key to the "on" position (just before you turn it all the way to start the car), does that mean you're out of oil? No. It means that something is wrong with the warning light itself. If the light doesn't work then, it's not going to work at all. Like when you need it, for example.

* * *

One more thing about oil: overfilling is just as bad as underfilling. Can you really have too much of a good thing? you ask. Yes. If you're half a quart or even a quart overfilled, it's not a big deal, and I wouldn't be afraid to drive the car under those circumstances. But if you're a quart and a half or two quarts or more overfilled, you could have so much oil in the crankcase that the spinning crankshaft is going to hit the oil and turn it into suds. It's impossible for the pump to pump suds, so you'll ruin the motor. It's kind of like a front-loading washing machine that goes berserk and spills suds all over the floor when you put too much detergent in. That's what happens to your motor oil when you overfill it.

With all this talk about things that can go wrong, let's not forget that modern engines are pretty incredible. People always say, "You know, the cars of yesteryear were wonderful. They built cars rough and tough and durable in those days."

Horsefeathers.

The cars of yesteryear were nicer to look at because they were very individualistic. They were all different, and some were even beautiful. In fact, when I was a kid, you could tell the year, make, and model of a car from a hundred paces just by looking at the taillights or the grille.

Nowadays, they all look the same. They're like jelly-beans on wheels. You can't tell one from the other. But the truth is, they've never made engines as good as they make them today. Think of the abuse they take! None of the cars of yesteryear was capable of going 60 or 70 miles per hour all day long and taking it for 100,000 miles.

Engines of today—and by today I mean from the late '60s on up—are far superior. What makes them superior is not only the design and the metallurgy, but the lubricants. The oil they had thirty years ago was lousy compared to what we have today. There are magic additives and detergents and long-chain polymers and what-have-you that make them able to hold dirt in suspension and to neutralize acids and to lubricate better than oils of the old days.

There aren't too many things that will go wrong, because the engines are made so well and the tolerances are closer. And aside from doing stupid things like running out of oil or failing to heed the warning lights or overfilling the thing, you shouldn't worry.

But here's one word of caution about cars that have timing belts: Lots of cars these days are made with overhead camshafts. The camshaft, which opens the valves, is turned by a gear and gets its power from the crankshaft. Many cars today use a notched rubber *timing belt* to connect the two shafts instead of a chain because it's cheaper and easy to change. And here's the caveat: *if you don't change it and the belt breaks, it can mean swift ruin to the engine.* The pistons can hit the valves and you'll have bent valves and possibly broken pistons.

So you can do many hundreds of dollars' worth of damage by failing to heed the manufacturer's warning about changing the timing belt in a timely manner. No pun intended. For most cars, the timing belt replacement is somewhere between $100 and $200. It's not a big deal.

I might add that there are many cars that have rubber timing belts that will *not* cause damage to the engine when they break. But even if you have one of those cars, make sure that you get the belt changed, at the very least, when the manufacturer suggests it. If there's no specific recommendation and you have a car with a rubber belt, we would recommend that you change it at 60,000 miles. Because even if you don't do damage to the motor when the belt breaks, you're still going to be stuck somewhere, maybe somewhere unpleasant. Maybe even Cleveland! So you want to make sure that you don't fall into that situation.

Many engines that have rubber timing belts also use the belt to drive the water pump. On these, don't forget to change the water pump when you change the timing belt, because the leading cause of premature belt failure is that the water pump seizes. So if you have a timing belt that drives the water pump, get the water pump out of there at the same time. You don't want to put a belt in and then have the water pump go a month later, because it'll break the new belt and wreck the engine.

The best way to protect all the other pieces that you can't get to without spending a lot of money is through frequent oil changes. The manufacturers recommend oil changes somewhere between seven and ten thousand miles, depending upon the car. We've always recommended that you change your oil at 3,000 miles. We realize for some people that's a bit of an inconvenience, but look at it as cheap insurance. And change the filter every time too.

And last but not least, I want to repeat this because it's important: Make sure your warning lights work. The oil pressure and engine temperature warning lights are your engine's lifeline. Check them every day. You should make it as routine as checking to see if your zipper's up. You guys should do it at the same time.

What you do is, you get into the car, check to see that your zipper's up, and then turn the key on and check to see if your oil pressure and temperature warning lights come on.

I don't know what women do.

Burning Oil

CLACK: Welcome to *Car Talk*.

My boyfriend tells me to get rid of my Volkswagen because it's starting to use oil. I don't get it. Aren't cars supposed to use oil? Help me out, because he makes me feel stupid.

CLACK: Your problem is with your boyfriend, not your car. You need a new boyfriend.

CLICK: Look at it this way. Your car's engine takes in air and gas—sucks it in through the carburetor—compresses it with a piston, lights it with a spark plug, and uses the power of the explosion to move a whole bunch of cranks, wheels, gears, and shafts.

CLACK: All of which make you go.

CLICK: Now, the oil is used to lubricate all those wheels and pistons and cranks and shafts. When people say the car is "using oil" or "burning oil," what they mean is that the oil, which is in there lubricating these myriad moving parts, is slipping past the pistons or the valves and burning up with the gasoline.

CLACK: Creating the dreaded blue smoke.

CLICK: Oil can also leak out through seals and cracks.

CLACK: Causing the ugly black spots on the garage floor. Or the living room floor, if you park your car in the house like my brother does.

CLICK: All this is a function of wear. As the engine wears out, it begins to use oil. Eventually, it has to be rebuilt or replaced. How many miles on your VW?

About 96,000.

CLACK: That's about when it starts. The oil leaks past the rings, which are supposed to seal the pistons. How much does it use?

I have to put in a quart every hundred miles or so.

CLICK: Oh, jeez! That's a lot! You're burning almost as much oil as gasoline. Oil is cheap, compared to $1,000 or so for a ring job or an engine rebuild. But when your engine is that worn, something else is probably about to go.

CLACK: Plus you're polluting the atmosphere. You can always get a new car, but can we get a new atmosphere?

CLICK: I hate to say it, but your boyfriend is right. Which VW do you have?

It's an old bug.

CLICK: Then you're lucky. You have an engine that's fairly cheap to rebuild.

CLACK: You still need a new boyfriend. If this guy likes to make you feel stupid, replace him at the same time.

Quantum Mechanics

CLICK: Hello, you're on *Car Talk.*

Hi, I'm calling from New York State and I have an '82 Volkswagen Quantum—

CLICK: And you can't find any Quantum mechanics?

Well, not exactly. This winter, it started to use oil. A lot of it.

CLACK: How much is a lot?

About a quart every two weeks.

CLICK: What's that in miles? How much do you drive?

I do about 200 miles a week.

CLICK: That comes out to a quart every 400 miles.

It doesn't have blue smoke. I would never know I burn oil at all.

CLICK: You wouldn't see blue smoke. Not at this rate.

CLACK: How many miles on this jalopy?

Just over 100,000.

CLACK: Aw, come one, give us a break, will you! Of course it's burning oil.

CLICK: How often do you change the oil?

Ah, maybe, like twice a year?

CLICK: Twice a year! And you drive 20,000 miles a year? Every 10,000 miles you change your oil?

Yeah, I think so.

CLACK: You should be ashamed of yourself. It's a wonder that you've gotten 100,000 out of this thing.

CLICK: If you had been conscientious, you could have probably gotten 200,000 miles out of this VW. That would have been some punishment, huh?

The only question I have is—well, it never had much power, but it has hardly any now. Is that because of the oil? I had a compression test done, and it was 165, all around.

CLICK: The oil consumption has nothing to do with power.

CLACK: The car's getting old. It's possible that your injectors are plugged up, or worn out. You need to use low-cholesterol gasoline. Ask for it at your dealer. Anyway, you're getting tired of the car. You're looking for a car with more power, I can tell. You're ready for a Saab.

No, not for a couple more years.

CLACK: A couple more years? Okay, buy a case of oil, and carry it around in the back. Don't worry about it.

CLICK: But you should change the oil more frequently. Like every 3,000 miles.

CLACK: Change it every 3,000 miles, and instead of burning a quart every 500 you'll start burning a quart every 1,000.

Thanks.

CLACK: That is a testimony to German engineering. The lady has changed her oil ten times in the past five years—and the car still runs!

The Greatest Invention Since the Pop Top

I have two oil questions. What does 10W30 mean? And what does the red light on the dashboard tell you?

CLACK: Those numbers refer to the viscosity, or thickness, of the oil. Oil thins out when it gets hot, and thickens when it's cold, like molasses. In cold weather you want a thinner oil, so that your starter won't have such a hard time turning your engine over. Then when it's hot you want it to stay thick enough to keep everything lubricated. Oil that stays thin when it's cold (10 weight) and thick when it's hot (30 weight), is called multiple-viscosity oil.

CLICK: For Alaska they have 5–20; for Florida they have 20–50. Around here (Boston) 10–30's fine.

What kind of oil should I buy for my car? Can I mix brands?

CLACK: It depends on what kind of car you have. If you drive a Lambofarrighettilini X-765Y with a turbo-wankeldiesel, you need a specially formulated racing oil. Otherwise, don't worry about it. Pennzoil, Quaker State, Valvoline—they're all about the same and they're all plenty good enough.

CLICK: Oil cans have letters on the back which rate it, like SE, CC. Don't worry about what they mean, just buy one with the greatest number of letters.

CLACK: Seriously, the letters represent the quality rating of the oil, with the best currently rated as SG for gas engines and CD for diesels.

CLICK: And don't believe that old wives' tale about how you can't mix brands of oil. It's nonsense. I don't have to tell you who made it up, do I?

My other question was about the red light on the dash. The oil light. What does it mean, exactly?

CLICK: It means stop!

CLACK: It means pray!

CLICK: That light should say $2,500. Then people would pull over when it came on.

It means the oil is low?

CLACK: Sometimes, but not always. What it monitors is oil *pressure*. The oil is pumped through the engine and has to be under pressure to lubricate well. When the light comes on, it means the oil is either gone or not being pumped enough to lubricate the bearings. It means you

have ten seconds until Total Destruct . . . nine . . . eight
. . . seven . . .

CLICK: Sometimes on an old engine, the oil light will
flicker when you're idling. This means the engine is worn,
and a little oil is leaking out around the bearings. There's
not much you can do about it. But if it comes on or stays
on when an engine is running at speed, it means *shut
down.* You can turn a $2,000 engine into a $1.25 hunk of
scrap iron in a very few seconds without oil. I know. I've
done it to my brother's car!

The Last Studebaker

CLICK: Hello, you're on *Car Talk.*

*Hi, this is Jim, calling from Arlington, Texas. I'm worried
that my Studebaker engine is dying.*

CLICK: Uh-oh. What year?

It's a '62. A V-8 Hawk.

CLICK: Gee, what a great motor!

CLACK: Notice, he didn't say great car.

CLICK: No. Great motor, though.

*Well, the car's doing pretty well, but the motor's a little tired
now. It takes about a quart of oil to go to Dallas and back.*

CLACK: How far is that?

That's about 70 miles, round trip.

CLICK: That's pretty bad. That's serious oil consumption.

Yeah. And if you step on it real hard, it seems like it doesn't run on all cylinders. Anyway, I was wondering if there's not a way to put another, more popular engine in it. I thought maybe you guys had some experience with that and could tell me what would fit.

CLACK: You mean, experience with putting junkyard engines in Studebaker Hawks? Oh yeah, we do two or three a week.

CLICK: In other words, you want us to say, "Yeah, throw in a Chevy 350. Move the mounts up six inches."

Yeah.

CLICK: Actually, you can go to a junkyard, and they'll tell you what fits. Probably nothing does without some modification. But look, before you do this, how many miles are on this car?

I got it from a doctor who got it from one of his patients who died and didn't pay him—

CLACK: Ungrateful wretch!

So all I know is that it has 97,000 on the odometer. But I found all these old receipts from California, and they show it had 70,000 ten years ago—

CLICK: So it's probably 197,000. Still, if the body's not too bad—

It's not bad. I know what you're going to say. I thought of maybe rebuilding it.

CLACK: Do you like the 289, the Studebaker engine?

Well, I like it. It's better than a sharp stick in the eye.

CLICK: Well, then rebuilding it would be the smarter thing to do. It would still be a collector's item. But only do it if you can find somebody to do it right. Don't cut any corners.

CLACK: Otherwise, put a Chevy 350 in it. Seriously. You can make it fit. Put in the engine and transmission, and you'll have a more trouble-free car.

CLICK: But not such a collector's item, of course . . .

CLACK: Who's going to know? Who looks under the hood? They'll see him in that Studie and they'll all say: "Here he comes, there he goes!"

Timing Chain

Hi, this is Steve, from Massachusetts. I have an '87 Dodge Caravan, one of the small vans.

CLICK: Good for you!

With 57,000 miles on it. Love the car.

CLACK: We have exactly that many miles on our Caravan. They all have 57,000.

Anyway, I noticed a sort of, you know, click and clack tapping noise, so I took it to the dealer to get the valves adjusted, and they said the words "timing chain."

CLICK: And you quaked in your boots.

Well, yeah! Then they said $900.

CLACK: And you said, "Praise the Lord!"

Something like that. Anyway, I've got a few questions. First, isn't this normally too soon for something like this to happen?

CLICK: Yes. Next question.

How serious is it?

CLICK: Financially or medically? In terms of the three kinds of problems you can have with your car, yours is somewhere between Two and Three. In other words, it's your pocketbook, not your life, that's in jeopardy.

I've got a 50,000-mile warranty. If I moan about it to the Chrysler service representative, do you think they'll help me out?

CLACK: With 57,000 miles? You're dreaming. I think their response will probably be something like "Ha!" or "Gotcha!" Or they may come right out and tell you, "That was supposed to go 6,000 miles ago, at 51,000."

CLICK: Yeah, but even so, $900 is way out of line.

Really? They're saying $600 parts, $300 labor.

CLACK: What's $600? The timing chain? Did they give you the list?

CLICK: I would ask for the written estimate. First of all, maybe they're planning to do a lot more than the timing chain. Maybe all you heard is what they call the "key words."

CLACK: Before you passed out.

They were talking about replacing gears, timing gears.

CLICK: Even so, there's no $600 worth of parts there. My guess is the whole job is probably less than half of that.

Oh boy!

CLICK: Don't get happy yet! There may be more to the job than you told us about. There may be a lot of other things that are gone. But if it's running well otherwise, and it's just noisy, then I would shop around and try to get a better price.

One last question, then. Do you think I should get the job done, or should I trade the car? I love the car.

CLICK: What kind of question is that? If you like it, fix it. It almost never pays to trade.

CLACK: You know what it's worth?

My guess is around $4,500, if I sell it myself.

CLACK: Oh, it's worth a little bit more than that. But do you know what a new one costs? Take a stab.

$14,000?

CLICK: Keep stabbing. Stab higher. $19K fully loaded. You know how many timing chains you can do for nineteen grand? You can do one a week; even at $600 apiece, God forbid, you can do more than thirty.

When I buy a car, I want to keep it for ten years, so I just—

CLACK: You got it, man! That is the only way to do it. Ten years is the absolute minimum. You're well on your way to keeping this car for ten years, if you can squeeze another eight out of it.

Battle of the Tin Cans

Hello, what do you think of Oldsmobiles? I've got an '85, a Firenza. The first thing in the morning when I start the car, it sounds like a bunch of men under there throwing tin cans at each other; it just clatters unbelievably. I called the dealer and they said, "Bring it in." But by the time I get to the dealers, the noise has quit.

CLACK: How long does it take for the noise to quit?

Oh, just a minute or two, then it's gone.

CLICK: Well, the first thing that comes to mind is that you have a bad oil pump.

CLACK: Either you have a weak oil pump, or you have worn parts in your engine, like crankshaft bearings, or connecting-rod bearings; or you might have the wrong-viscosity oil in there, either too high or too low. The beginning of this sound, did it come with an oil change, for example?

No, it seemed to be with the weather.

CLACK: And it got gradually worse?

Yeah, it's worse than ever. I mean, I wake up the neighbors taking off in the morning.

CLICK: What you should do is leave the car overnight with your Oldsmobile dealer.

I did! And they said, "We didn't hear anything." Really. That's the truth.

CLICK: You might want to go someplace else, then. If they think that they will have to honor something on warranty, they might be playing stupid.

So what could happen?

CLACK: Plenty. If the oil pump is not working, you'll wreck the engine. You got $2,000 you don't need?

Well . . .

CLACK: I didn't think so. The point is, there is something wrong. It could be something unimportant, like a loose heat shield on your exhaust. But you need to find out what it is.

CLICK: Take it to another garage, get the so-called second opinion.

CLACK: We come with the second opinion. The second opinion is the one we give first. Then we give the first opinion.

CLICK: Which is that it's low oil pressure. Take it someplace else, and tell them that you would like them to listen to it on a cold start in the morning, and moreover, to check your oil pressure.

Okay.

CLICK: Cold and hot. It could be something simple like a cracked pulley. There are a million things it could be, but a discerning ear will figure it out. Unfortunately, we can't help you any more than that.

CLACK: Unless you want to call us in the morning when you start the car, and hold the phone under the hood.

The Cheapskate

CLICK: Hello, you're on *Car Talk*. Speak now or forever hold your peace.

I have an '85 and '86 Mitsubishi Galant.

CLACK: Make up your mind. An '85 or an '86?

I have both of them. One of each! One for her, one for me.

CLACK: What a guy! Who's got the new one?

She has the new one.

CLICK: A gentleman! There are so few of us left, you know? So what's wrong with these things?

They run beautifully. But the manual says that the jet valve should be adjusted every 15,000 miles. What is the jet valve, and does it really need to be adjusted at $60 a throw with taxes every 15,000 miles?

CLACK: The jet valve is an auxiliary intake valve. Your cars have three valves per cylinder. And they say you should adjust the jet valve how often?

Every 15,000 miles.

CLICK: And what about the other valves?

That's all it says. Jet-valve adjustment, 15,000 miles. That makes it an expensive proposition.

CLACK: Well, don't forget, there are four of these jet valves. It's not $60 per valve, it's $60 for the whole job.

CLICK: How many miles do you drive in a year?

About 12,000.

CLACK: So every fifteen months, you're going to spend sixty bucks, and you're complaining about it? C'mon!

Well, it's just that the engines are running so beautifully without the adjustment, and—

CLICK: And you think they're going to keep running like that forever if you don't take care of them?

What happens if they're not adjusted?

CLICK: They burn. If any valve goes unadjusted for a long period of time, you get what's called valve seat recession; the valve adjustment can become too tight, and you'll burn the valve out. The valves are exposed to the combustion. And if they overheat and melt, the engine's going to have bad compression on that cylinder.

CLACK: Right. And then it's going to cost you—

I know, I know. Hundreds.

CLICK: Don't be a cheapskate. Remember Click and Clack's Axiom Number 1314: "It's the Stingy Person Who Spends the Most."

CLACK: Thanks for your call. . . . He probably wouldn't have called if it had been his dime.

Pray for a Leak

CLACK: Hello, you're on *Car Talk*.

Hi, this is Carol from Austin, Texas. I've got a question about my 1982 BMW 320i. I looked around trying to get a good used car and that's what I bought. And I change the oil real frequently, every 3,000 miles, and I drive like 2,000 miles every month. So I change it a lot. The last couple of oil changes, I noticed that I had only a quart left and that was it. I had not noticed any oil spots under the car or any blue smoke behind it. I was just wondering, where did the oil go?

CLICK: How many miles on this car?

There are 75,000 miles on it.

CLICK: And you bought the car with how many miles on it?

About 65,000.

CLACK: What highway do you drive on?

What highway?

CLACK: Yeah. What number? What route number?

Interstate 35 usually, I guess. Why?

CLACK: That's where your oil is. It'll be a long, skinny puddle. That is, if you're lucky. If you're leaking it.

What do you mean, lucky?

CLACK: Because usually leaks are less expensive to fix than oil burning. But you shouldn't be burning, not with only 75K on this car, unless the person who drove it for the first 65,000 miles was a meatball.

CLICK: Which is very likely. I'll bet whoever owned this BMW 320i before you didn't drive it as gently as you are driving it.

You're saying he might have driven it like a maniac.

CLICK: You said it, not me. Look for a leak first. But the fact that you can't find a puddle under the car doesn't mean that it's not leaking. It may be leaking only when it's running.

CLACK: In fact, that's more likely—when the oil's hot and under pressure. I mean, have you ever just let the engine run for a few hours, in one spot, with something under the car?

CLICK: Like a newspaper.

CLACK: Or a husband.

CLICK: Just let it idle in one place on a nice piece of dry, clean pavement. Better yet, take it to a mechanic and let him get dirty.

Okay.

CLACK: She likes that idea. Yeah. And say, "Where's my leak?" It could be anything. What if your oil filter isn't tight? What if your oil-pressure sending unit is broken? You would be throwing oil out while you were driving, but as soon as you shut the engine off, it would stop leaking, because the oil would all be down at the bottom instead of up there where the hole is. So it would never show any puddle.

CLICK: Pray for that. It's ten bucks for a new oil switch. If you're not lucky—

CLACK: Ten bucks? This is a BMW we're talking about! It costs ten bucks on a BMW just to put air in the tire. That special German air—

The Slant Six

Hi, I'm Phyllis, from Hartford.

CLACK: Hi, Phyllis. How're you doing?

Not bad. I'm looking for a new car. I'm calling about engines. For years I've been hearing about slant-six engines.

CLICK: You missed it by about a decade, Phyllis!

CLACK: Oh, Phyllis, where've you been?! The slant six went out with knickers.

I heard you can still get one, though. And I heard it was a great engine.

CLACK: It was, in its day. Those Conestoga wagons were great in their day too.

But they still work. The slant sixes, I mean.

CLICK: Yeah, but there aren't any new cars that have them.

That I figured. What I want to know is, what should I look for in the new engines? I have no idea what to look for in an engine.

CLACK: This is a heavy question! You want something with that same degree of reliability as the slant six, in other words?

Yes.

CLICK: Why?

Why not?

CLICK: The body won't last that long. If the body won't last twenty years, why make an engine that'll last twenty years? That's what they have figured out.

CLACK: Yeah. You gotta have planned obsolescence so that everything wears out at the same time. About when the ashtray gets filled. What kind of a car do you like? What have you been eyeing?

The Dodge Colt, Mazda 323, Toyota Tercel, that class.

CLICK: Gee. You might as well throw in a Suzuki Samurai, as long as you're down here with the death traps.

CLACK: So you like these little cars? That's all right. We won't try to talk you out of it, not this go-round. Are you going to be doing most of your driving on I-91, or are you going to be tooling around Hartford all day?

Tooling around, yes. What about the Novas? I liked them, but I hear they're not going to be made anymore.

CLACK: They're going to be made, but they have a new name. The Nova is now the Geo Prizm.

CLICK: They couldn't sell them in South America, because Nova means "doesn't go" in Spanish. *No va.* So they had trouble with that name. Bad vibes, you know.

But getting back to engines. Is there a difference in engines today? Is there something that one should look for?

CLICK: Engines today are better than engines ever have been, believe it or not.

CLACK: The trouble with the engines today is that they're nowhere near as good as engines used to be.

CLICK: Now that we've gotten that straightened out— the cars you've mentioned, the Colt, the 323, the Tercel, they all have wonderful engines. They're all underpowered, but the cars are all undersized, so it works out okay.

You're saying there's nothing today that can even touch the slant six?

CLICK: Oh, these are better!

Come on.

CLICK: No, it's true. In terms of reliability and durability, they are better.

Even with the aluminum?

CLICK: Don't worry about aluminum. I mean, after all, beer cans have been made out of aluminum for a couple of decades now, and they don't wear out.

CLACK: Phyllis, what's the basic question? Why do you want to know about this? Should you be shopping for an engine as opposed to shopping for a car?

Well—

CLICK: We're not being facetious here. Some people went out and bought slant-six engines. They didn't care what it was in, as long as it was a slant six.

CLACK: And they were putting them in things like Aspens and Volares. And it was a clear case of the engine being too good for the car.

Why was that? Was it true that gravity had something to do with its efficiency?

CLACK: The slant? No, nothing. The slant had to do with the design of the hood. They wanted to lower the hood angle, so they leaned the engine over. There was no mysticism or magic here at all.

CLICK: So you can buy any of these new cars and, truthfully, their engines, if taken care of, are just as good if not better than the slant six. They're more efficient, and they'll take you 100,000 miles plus.

CLACK: And by then you're ready to junk the little thing because you're sick of sitting in it and your back hurts. That's it, Phyllis. Thanks for your call.

6

ELECTRICITY—THE FINAL FRONTIER

Captain Kirk was wrong. Space is not the final frontier. Electricity is. Everyone knows what space is. But *no one* knows what electricity is. Even the inventor of electricity, Don Ameche, doesn't know what electricity is. Some people, however, do know what it *does*. And here at Car Talk Plaza, in the Click and Clack Astronuclear High Energy Physics Lab and Coffee Shop, we have determined not only what it does, but *how* it does it. (Eat your hearts out, Pons and Fleischman!)

Below is an abstract of a paper recently submitted to *Scientific American* (and also to the *National Enquirer*, in case *Scientific American* turns out to be a bunch of stiffs).

WHAT IS ELECTRICITY?

Take a battery. Make it a car battery. If you hook it up in the following way, you can make a light bulb light.

What makes it light, you may ask? Well, inside the battery there are these "little guys" who run from the battery to the light and turn it on. And boy, do they run fast! I mean, they're at that light bulb before you can say piston puss! (Some people refer to the flow of electrons or some such thing. These people are to be avoided. They are wackos who will lead you astray and take your money.) In our lab, we have carefully studied the behavior and habits of the little guys, and now we are prepared to reveal the details of their behavior.

One peculiarity of the little guys is that (unlike us) they are extremely industrious; they will work until they drop from exhaustion, if you ask them to. If you hooked things up correctly and went away for the weekend, those little guys would keep that light burning until you got back on Monday (or till they all dropped from exhaustion, whichever came first).

Another significant finding from our research is that they consider the battery to be their home, and although they are more willing to work for you, they will not leave home (the battery) unless they are absolutely certain that they can get home again. Since they only travel through metals (like wires), it's necessary to hook things up correctly; that is,

1. a route (wire) from the *exit* door to the light.
2. a return route (wire) from the light back to the *entrance* door.

(Some people call the exit door the *positive terminal* of
the battery and the entrance door the *negative terminal*.)

Notice the flaps on the doors? They open only one
way. So the little guys can only go out the exit door and
back through the entrance door. Strange, huh? It means
that they only travel in one direction. Out the exit door,
over to the light, and back through the entrance door. We
tried tricking the little guys. For example, we tried putting something between the entrance door and the wire
(like a piece of spaghetti, which looks like wire, but, of
course, isn't).

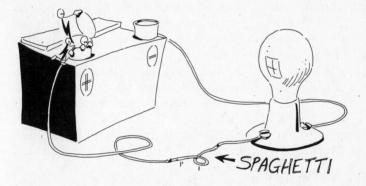

← SPAGHETTI

Not a one of them was fooled. We know, because the
light did not go on. Somehow, they can see all the way
around the loop and if there's no way home, they *will not
leave!* (Some literature in less scientific journals has referred to this phenomenon as the need for a "complete
circuit." That's fine. If they want to call it that, it's no
skin off our noses. We have no axes to grind. We have no
fish to fry. Yes, we even have no bananas.)

Actually, we have been able to use this peculiarity to
our advantage. Let's face it; sometimes you don't want a
light to stay on all night. So all you need to do is "break
the circuit" and the light will go off.

Of course, you can break the circuit anyplace and it
will always work the same way because these little guys

can *always* tell when there isn't a way to get home. In the words of one of our senior research scientists, "This is neat."

Since this gave us the ability to switch the light on and off, we called this little device the "switcheroo." The people in the lab shortened it to "switch."

Here's another interesting thing. And it makes a lot of sense to us, from our personal experiences. It's this: Some jobs are harder than others; and harder jobs require more little guys than easy jobs. For example, we found that it takes only one little guy to light a dome light. But it takes ten or fifteen of them to light up the powerful high-beam headlights. And, *get this:* To turn the starter motor takes 150 to 200 of them! (Incidentally, this may explain some confusion in the literature. The scientists who agree with us that there are little guys who are doing all this work have sometimes thought that the little guys were ants! It does make sense; ants *are* industrious little fellows, like our little guys. To add to the confusion, some people have misspelled ants and it has appeared in some literature as *amps*. Like "it takes one *amp* (instead of one *ant*) to light the dome light" or "the starter requires 150 *amps*." We're pretty sure this is a misspelling of "ants." In any event, it's irrelevant to this discussion, because we're using the more accepted terminology of "little guys." If you want to call them "amps," fine.)

Of course, when there's a big job that requires a lot of guys, it helps to give them all enough room to get to where they're going. If you don't, those industrious little guys will all try to cram through any available passageway. For example, we once asked them to turn the big heavy starter motor and provided only a little skinny passageway for them (i.e., a skinny wire). Well, 150 of those little guys came scrambling out to turn that motor. They all crowded together in that little wire, bumping into each other in their zeal to get the job done. All the friction of those hot little bodies bumping together finally melted the wire. It would have been a real catastrophe if we hadn't been around to disconnect things!

We reached two important conclusions from that potential disaster. The first, of course, was to make sure that we provide fat wires when lots of guys are required to do a job. And the second was that we found a way to prevent a disaster by putting a little device in the wire that would melt and break the circuit *before* the wire got hot enough to melt. It's called a fuse.

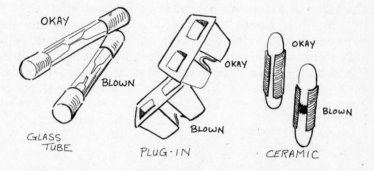

By the way, we also found a way to save a lot of wire. Let's say we wanted to light up a bulb at the back of the car—a taillight. Normally, we'd do it like this:

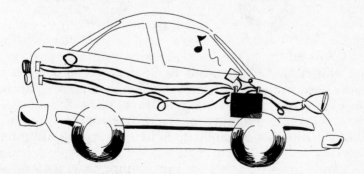

We'd have to run a wire from the exit door (plus side, or positive terminal) of the battery to the bulb. We'd also probably put in a switch and maybe even a fuse for safety's sake. Then we'd run another wire from the bulb to the entrance door of the battery (negative). Then for the other taillight we'd do it again. And yet again for the backup lights, the brake lights. I mean, we're talking about a lot of wire! In fact, we ran out of wire. So we all started looking for another piece of wire to run from the taillight back to the battery, when one of our research assistants, Polly Unsaturates, pointed out: "Hey, dweebs! We already *have* a conductor running from the back of the car to the front of the car. It's *the car itself.*"

You talk about a Eureka-type experience! I mean, the excitement in the lab was, well, exciting. Of course, Polly was right. Talk about not seeing the forest for the trees. The whole car is metal, so why not use the car for a wire?

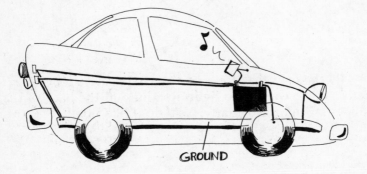

GROUND

Notice that at the front of the car we just connect a short wire from the entrance door to some metal part of the car. At the rear end we do the same thing. In between, the car itself is the route for the little guys. And you talk about a route! Wow, the car is like a superhighway for them.

And we can do this for everything. Now, instead of *two* wires for everything, we only need one. Like for the radio? Just one wire goes *to* the radio and then the radio is connected to anything (metal) on the car and those little guys will find their way back home. For some reason, people call this *grounding* the radio or *grounding* the taillight. And they call the entrance door and all metal parts of the car the *ground*. I never did understand that. But if that's what they want to call it, it's okay by us. It's no skin off our noses. We have no axes to grind. We have no fish to fry. You know the rest.

That's about it. We mentioned earlier that the little guys *do* get tired. But luckily, we don't need them to work all the time. In fact, we really only need them to *start* the car. Once the engine is running, we can use the spinning motion (again!) to actually *create* more of the little guys in a device called a *generator* or *alternator*. The janitor at Car Talk Plaza actually figured this out; a guy named Mike Fardy or something like that. (My brother tells me it's Faraday; he should know, since he has applied for the guy's job.)

Anyway, what happens is that once the car is started, we immediately start generating more electricity and we use this newly generated stuff to run everything that needs electricity while the engine is running—lights, radio, rear-window defogger, microwave oven. If we don't make enough, the little guys in the battery are always ready and willing to make up the difference. And if we make too much, we send these fresh new recruits into the battery and the older tired guys go to a well-deserved retirement.

With this background, you should be able to answer just about any electricity-related question. Here are a few real ones.

The Ground Strap

CLICK: Hello, you're on *Car Talk*. . . .

This is Jim. I'm calling from Wisconsin.

CLICK: Hi, Jim.

I have a problem with my 1980 Chevy Citation. I'm getting low voltage, so when I have the lights on, they're not very bright. And when I have other electrical things on, such as the windshield wipers or the radio, you can obviously see that there's not enough power to do the job.

CLACK: Have you paid your electric bill?

I've had the alternator checked, and they say the output is fine. The belt has been checked, and it's tight. The mysterious thing is that when I wiggle the stick-shift lever, the lights brighten and then dim again, and you can kind of keep them flashing brighter and dimmer that way. Also, another curious thing is, if I press the clutch just a little bit, not to fully disengage it—

CLICK: The same thing happens.

Right.

CLACK: And the reason it's happening is that you have a ground wire that's supposed to go from the chassis to the block—

CLICK: And it's gone!

CLACK: It's broken. Whoever tested your alternator didn't test it correctly. Because if he had tested it, he would've gotten the same information that we just got over the phone. It can't be charging *enough*.

CLICK: And the reason that stepping on the clutch pedal makes it charge is that the clutch cable and the throw-out bearing are acting as the ground. You see, with all the different circuits in the car, the frame of the car is the ground; it completes the circuit. But the alternator grounds through the engine, which is connected to the frame only by these rubber mounts; so it doesn't ground, or doesn't ground very well—until you step on the clutch or wiggle the lever, which makes it connect. You're completing the circuit, see?

Yeah.

CLICK: Interesting, huh? But there is supposed to be a ground strap between the body and the motor. Replace it or reconnect it, and you'll be all set.

CLACK: Or better still, don't even look for it. Just put a new one on.

All right. So there's not a switch or something.

CLICK: No, it's the ground strap. Absolutely. This car was probably involved in an accident, or they pulled the motor out and forgot to hook the strap back up. It appeared probably relatively unimportant at the time. "Say, Billy, you forgot that strap." "Ah, that's nothing." "Does everything work?" "Yeah, everything works." "Then it can't be important. Get this beast out of here."

I'll check it out. Thanks.

CLACK: Let us know if it works.

CLICK: Better yet, let us know if it doesn't work.

CLACK: Better yet, don't let us know if it doesn't work.

The Light Switch

This is Teresa from Brooklyn. I've got a little problem with my Pinto. The headlights start to go on and off after driving it ten minutes.

CLACK: Good. Great. That's a safety feature. It means you've gone far enough in this old clunker.

CLICK: Yeah, you're not supposed to drive a Pinto at night.

I thought maybe it was a fuse or something, but when I pull into my driveway and turn off the ignition, the lights continue to flash on and off.

CLACK: What's wrong with it is the headlight switch. There is no fuse per se for the headlights. The headlight switch itself is the headlight fuse; it's a circuit breaker. And what's happening is it's heating up and the circuit opens and the lights go off. Then it cools off and the lights go back on.

Where is that located?

CLACK: It's part of the switch that you pull on the dashboard when you turn the lights on. The switch is like ten bucks. It comes out the back. You have to get the pull knob off, and you have to reach around up under the dashboard and press a little button. . . .

Sounds complicated.

CLACK: Take it to the corner gas station. Say, "Please change my headlight switch." And they'll say, "Why? The lights work fine." And say, "Ah, that's all right. I change it every month anyway, whether it needs it or not." Then they'll do it cheap, hoping they'll get all this crazy woman's business. But that's what the problem is.

Great. I was so puzzled, and I thought, well, I'll try them with this problem. We had it in to a mechanic one time and he had the car running for two hours and nothing happened.

CLICK: All he did was burn up your gas. It isn't the engine that's causing it, it's the switch. Tell him to put a new switch in. Like I said, it's ten bucks for the part.

CLACK: It's probably twenty. My brother lives in the past. Thanks for your call.

The Nonstarter

CLICK: Hello, you're on *Car Talk*.

Hello. This is Sarah from Greenwich, Connecticut.

CLACK: Hi, Sarah. What's up?

I have a 1982 Toyota Corolla and I got into it one morning last summer and I started it and then I turned off the engine to talk to a friend, and when I turned the key again, nothing happened. It was just total silence.

CLACK: Your friend couldn't think of anything to say?

No, I mean the car wouldn't do anything. I wiggled a few knobs and wondered what to do and after a while tried the key again, and it started up.

CLICK: What happened then? Does the car still do this?

Yes! It's happened probably a dozen times over the year. Weeks will go by, and the car runs fine, and then all of a sudden I'll turn the key and—nothing.

CLICK: You don't rob banks for a living, do you?

CLACK: If you do, leave the engine running. Don't shut this baby off if you have to make a quick getaway!

CLICK: What's going on is that the starter is going bad. We replace a lot of these gear-reduction starters on Toyotas. At some point in the late '70s, they went from a normal starter—

CLACK: A real starter.

CLICK: —to this kind of starter that you have, which is a gear-reduction type. Not to say that they're the only ones who did it. Chrysler has done it for years, but they have better luck with it.

So I need a new starter?

CLICK: You're getting an improper contact inside the solenoid, or there's a dead spot in the starter. If you just hold that key in the crank position, it'll eventually start. Also, a gentle rap with a hammer on the housing of the starter will get it to turn over.

CLACK: Are you crazy? She doesn't want to be sticking her hands down there starting the engine with a hammer! Don't listen to him. Get a new starter.

CLICK: But first, before you replace the starter, you should have your mechanic check out the connections at the battery, to make sure that they're good and tight and clean. There's a wire that runs from the battery to the starter motor. Make sure that's nice and clean and fastened securely. Also, check the little push-on connector from the ignition switch.

CLACK: And if it's not in the wiring, it's in the starter itself. And it's guaranteed to get worse. So get it fixed before you get stuck somewhere.

CLICK: Way out in East Overshoe, Connecticut. Or pulling out across three lanes of traffic, and it dies in the middle, and this semi comes bearing down on you—and you turn the key and it goes—gulp!

CLACK: You don't need that, so get a new starter.

Tomorrow.

More Shocking Truth

CLACK: Hello, you're on *Car Talk.*

My name is Mary. I'm from Los Angeles. I'm calling about my windshield wipers. I think the fuse is blown, because nothing's happening. Can I change the fuse myself? I'm afraid to get shocked.

CLICK: You called the right guys. We never shock anybody. Nothing but the dullest stuff here.

CLACK: What are you driving?

A Ford Taurus.

CLACK: A nice car.

CLICK: What does it matter what she's driving?

CLACK: I just like to know. What color is it?

CLICK: Don't pay any attention to him. Here's the deal: Every driver should know where her fuse box is. It's different in every car, but your owner's manual will tell you.

CLACK: Or get the kid at the gas station to show you.

CLICK: Whatever. It'll be in some out-of-the-way spot under the dash.

CLACK: It'll look like this.

Like what?

CLACK: I'm holding one up.

CLICK: On a radio show?

CLACK: Well, I can't make the sound of one. They don't make any noise.

CLICK: Seriously, find out where it is, and yes, you can change it yourself. There's not enough electricity in any of these car circuits to shock you. Only the spark plug wires and the coil wire, under the hood, can shock you. Do you know how to spot a bad fuse?

CLACK: I'm holding one up.

Yes, they have a broken piece, right?

CLICK: Right. They all have a little wire or metal strip, and the bad one will be burned in half. That's the one you replace. Carry a box of extras; you can get them at any car-parts store. And if it blows more than once or twice, get it checked out, because that means something else is wrong.

And don't worry about being shocked?

CLICK: And don't worry about being shocked.

Size Ten Shoe

CLICK: Hello, you're on *Car Talk*.

I have a question about a radio in a Toyota.

CLICK: Sorry, we don't do radios.

CLACK: Toyotas have those backward radios. Isn't the on–off knob on the right?

Right. It's on the right.

CLACK: Well, that's my brother's department. I only handle radios with the on–off switch on the left.

CLICK: So go ahead.

Well, I'll tell you what it does. The volume goes way down and one light stays on, but the stereo light goes off.

CLICK: And you can still vaguely hear the station?

Yeah, if you turn it way up.

CLICK: You've got the same problem I have. You've lost one stage of amplification in the radio, and all you gotta do . . . What size shoe do you wear?

Huh?

CLICK: You wear a big shoe, like size ten? Give this baby a nice kick whenever it doesn't work and it'll come right back.

CLACK: Is this an AM–FM and cassette player all built into one?

No, it's just AM–FM.

CLACK: Just throw it away and buy another one.

Well, the other question I have is how to get it out. Does it fasten up behind the dashboard, or—

CLACK: Drive it to Boston and park on any street and leave the car unlocked, and those kids'll have that baby out in about thirty seconds.

CLICK: They should get jobs in all the radio shops. What kind of a Toyota is it?

It's a Corolla, a '79.

CLICK: Don't waste money on a radio. Keep kicking it. It'll keep working until you have to get rid of the car. I have two cars. Both of them have exactly the same problem. You gotta whack them to get them to work. Carry an old shoe on the dashboard.

CLACK: Sometimes I go driving in my brother's car, and after fifteen miles the radio just automatically comes on all by itself. It's a wonderful surprise.

That's what mine does too.

CLICK: See, that's good. You can listen to our show sometimes. Or just when they're about to tell you that we're under nuclear attack, you lose the radio.

CLACK: "This is a test. It is only a test. If it wasn't a test, you would be vapor by now."

Le Heap

My name is Ken and I'm calling from Erie, Pennsylvania. I have a Renault Le Car.

CLICK: We have a more endearing name for this vehicle, but you can call it Le Car if you'd like.

CLACK: Le Heap!

All right. It's a 1982—

CLICK: And you still have it?

Yes, it has only about 40,000 miles. I had another one, a 1980, and that gave me about 90,000 miles and not a drop of trouble.

CLACK: You bought two of these things?! You may be the only one on the planet to have done this.

Well, I had good luck with the 1980, so I bought the 1982.

CLICK: And you're not having such good luck with this one, are you?

Not with this one.

CLICK: See how the law of averages works? This is called, in statistics, the regression to the mean.

Yeah, probably.

CLICK: In our experience, these cars last about 60,000 miles. So if you get 90K out of the first one, 40K out of the second, what's the average? 60K.

No, about 65K.

CLICK: Well, whatever. You're over the limit! So anyway, what's the current problem with this thing, besides the fact that it won't start?

Well, that's the problem! How did you know? It's an electronic ignition; I checked everything, and the coil has been replaced. The module for the electronic ignition has been replaced. I put in a new battery, but still there's no spark.

CLACK: What does it do?

It cranks, it turns over, but there's no spark. I checked by taking the ignition coil wire out and grounding it, and it does not have any spark at all.

CLICK: You are sure that the distributor is, in fact, turning?

Well, I don't know whether I checked that or not.

CLICK: That's an important consideration. You can check it easily. Pull off the cap, and crank it, and see if the rotor is turning around.

Well, the guy at the dealership worked two days ago with the distributor, so I'm quite sure that he checked that.

CLACK: I wouldn't be too sure, but he probably did.

So now, why don't I have a spark?

CLICK: I don't know.

CLACK: You said you changed the pickup, you changed the coil, you changed the electronic ignition module—

Yes.

CLICK: And we're assuming that the distributor shaft turns.

CLACK: Must be a demon. Is there a witch in your neighborhood?

CLICK: You've done a continuity test on all the wires?

Yes.

CLICK: Well, it's conceivable that you can buy a faulty new part. You assume because you put these new parts in that they are all good, and it must be something else. But when everything else seems to be impossible—

CLACK: This is Sherlock Holmes talking now.

CLICK: Right. If nothing else fits, then it must be something that seems impossible.

Well, they won't take them back in the store. They don't take back the electronic parts.

CLICK: They won't give you your money back, but they will give you an exchange if you bring them back a faulty part. They'll just put it back on the shelf and sell it to the next guy that comes in.

CLACK: That's right, that's how you got it in the first place.

CLICK: They won't give you money, but they should exchange it if you're within the warranty period, which must be at least ninety days.

I see.

CLICK: If I had to guess out of all the pieces that you've replaced, I'd say it was the electronic ignition module. I'd try that one first.

I see.

CLACK: It happens. Make them take it back and at least test it.

The Louisville Slugger

CLICK: Hello, welcome to *Car Talk*. Where are you calling from, or from where are you calling, or whatever?

Berkeley, California. The problem we have is with a Datsun, a '77 pickup truck. You turn the starter to start the engine, and all you hear is a click.

CLICK: Do you hear a Click and a Clack, or just a click?

Just a click.

CLICK: Then you called the wrong show. Because this is Click and Clack.

Oh, well . . .

CLACK: So you hear a click. Then what? How do you get it started? You sit there and you keep monkeying with the key, right?

Yeah, you move the key back and forth and eventually it starts. But it didn't start today.

CLACK: So you called us. Okay, here's what you do. Get an assistant with a baseball bat.

CLICK: Not aluminum. Wood. Preferably a Louisville Slugger.

CLACK: Right. Now, you're gonna wield the bat while your assistant tries to start the car. Hopefully, it won't start. It'll do the same thing. It'll click. Now you gently rap the starter. Do you know where the starter is?

Yeah. Down at the bottom of the motor to one side at the rear.

CLACK: Good. It's at the end of the cable coming from the positive (plus) pole of the battery, that's another way to find it. You want to poise that baseball bat right above it as your partner is holding the key in the start position.

CLICK: Right. Makes sure he or she holds the key all the way over, then you whack it with the bat.

CLACK: Don't go for a home run. Just a single.

Hit the starter motor?

CLICK: You can hit the battery, too, if you want, if you're that angry. Why not take a few swings at the doors too! What the hell.

CLACK: No, don't hit the battery! Hit the starter motor. You want to give it a good thump. If it starts right up, then it's a bad starter. We've seen bad starters for many years in Nissans.

But you know, I've changed the starter four times.

CLACK: Yeah, and each time you buy one of those cheap rebuilts. You know what they do? They go to the junkyard and they pick up five hundred starters, and they test them all. They get one hundred that work and throw the rest away. Then they paint the one hundred and put them into boxes and they sell them as rebuilts.

Really? Rebuilt starters are not that hot, then.

CLICK: Some are excellent. But there are a lot of rebuilt starters that are not. Some cost forty bucks, which is what you're buying, aren't you? The truth now.

Well, yeah. So you want me to go out and buy a new starter?

CLICK: Not yet. We want you to do the test with the baseball bat first. If you whack it with the baseball bat and it doesn't start, then forget everything we've said!

CLACK: Right, call us next week.

CLICK: We'll go into the possibilities of the ignition key, the battery, the connections, and all that stuff. But probably it's the starter, which means that when you whack it with the bat, it'll start.

CLACK: In fact, just *show* it the bat. Maybe it'll get the hint.

Fill 'er Up

CLACK: Hello, you're on *Car Talk*.

Hi. I'm calling from Jamaica Plain, Massachusetts. I have a '77 Chevy Nova. And when I bought it the gas gauge wasn't working. I took it in to have someone look at it and they said they weren't sure what was wrong but it could cost as much as $300 or $400.

CLICK: It could. They're right about that.

CLACK: Don't fix it. Buy another '77 Nova for $300 or $400 and you'll have *hundreds* of spare parts.

Do they make any other kind of a gas gauge that I can use on it?

CLACK: Yeah. It's called a stick. You just stick it down there in the tank, through the hole, and you calibrate it. A yardstick works great.

CLICK: You want to know what it's most likely to be, and how to fix it?

Yeah.

CLICK: A bad fuel-tank sending unit. Even more likely is that the wire is disconnected. Or the ground is all rusted. There's a little wire that goes to this unit. It's connected to a variable resistor and as the float goes up and down inside the tank, the resistance changes, and that makes the gauge inside the car change. There are three things that can be broken. It can be the sending unit in the tank. It can be the wire between the sending unit and the dashboard. Or it can be the gauge in the dashboard.

Here's the way you figure it out. You should get a droplight, feel around up there, and you'll find this wire. If it's not connected, connect it. You're in luck. Everything's going to work. However, if it *is* connected, you pull it off.

CLACK: And you ground it to some spot on the chassis. Make sure you get a good ground. Have your trusty assistant in the car, with the key on, looking at the gauge. If the gauge goes all the way to full, then your problem is the sending unit in the tank. To drop the tank and replace the sending unit, you're talking maybe $100–$150.

CLICK: If the gauge doesn't do anything, then buy the yardstick.

Gee, a hundred bucks. I don't know.

CLICK: Look, you're the one who called. The cheapest way is just to fill up the tank every few days.

CLACK: Some people get nervous and they fill up the tank every day. Other people try to figure out how long they can go before filling up. Our father is one of those. His gas gauge went in his Chrysler, which got six miles to the gallon (on the highway!). So he multiplied six times the twenty gallons, which is what the tank held. And when he got to 119.5 miles, he started looking for a gas station.

CLICK: Except he didn't always make it. Maybe his choke stayed closed an extra thirty seconds on some cold day, or maybe he idled too long in traffic. . . .

7

FUEL SYSTEMS

Engines don't run on gasoline, they run on gasoline vapor mixed with air. If you take a paper cup full of gasoline (kids, don't try this at home!) and throw in a match, it'll put out the flame.

Well, it should have, anyway.

But if you put the gasoline in a Windex bottle and spray it out—*whoosh!* It'll light like crazy. So to make your car run, that's what you have to do. Take the gas that's in the tank, mix it with air, and shoot it into the cylinders. Whether it's done by carburetors or fuel injectors, it amounts to the same thing.

These are our two basic fuel-delivery systems. Once we've gotten the fuel from the tank by means of a pump of some kind, it enters the cylinders either through a carburetor or some kind of fuel-injection system. The purpose of both systems is to supply the correct mixture of fuel and air to the engine.

The problem is, carburetors are never better than close. Sometimes they run way too lean, sometimes they run way too rich. If they run too lean, the engine backfires and stalls, heats up and hesitates. If they run too rich, it pollutes the air and wastes a lot of gas.

For the first million years or so, this was okay. But as people began worrying about pollution, and gasoline became more expensive, carburetors became more and more complex, evolving into today's "feedback carburetor," which uses an under-the-hood computer chip and various sensors in order to reduce emissions.

In any event, there's no sense talking too much more about carburetors, because if you're buying a new car you're almost certain to get one with fuel injection. If you're not, you should be, because the truth is that, except for the really cheap little cars, no one is making cars with carburetors anymore. Carburetors are little dinosaurs.

Modern fuel injection also uses computer chips, but uses them more efficiently. What the computer does is take information from different sensors. There are temperature sensors that read both the air temperature and the engine-coolant temperature. There's a barometric-pressure sensor. There's another sensor that reads the manifold vacuum—that is, how much suction the engine is providing. Others note the throttle position, the engine speed and the vehicle speed, what gear the transmission is in, what color socks you're wearing. All this information is fed into the computer and used to run the fuel-injection system.

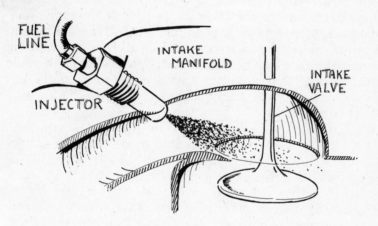

So, what is a fuel-injection system? What does it consist of?

There are several kinds. One is called a *multiport* or *multipoint fuel-injection* system, where you have an injector (a little squirter) for every cylinder. An electrical pulse is sent by the computer to each one of these injectors and shoots fuel in. The amount of fuel sent in is determined by the duration of the electrical pulse. When the engine is idling, it needs only a little fuel, and the pulse is shorter. When you're trying to outrun the cops, the pulse gets longer.

Pretty simple, huh? But you couldn't do this without a sophisticated computer to really monitor everything that's going on and send the signals, which are changing many times a second, to the fuel injectors.

Another type of system is what's called central fuel injection or *throttle body fuel injection.*

Now, each fuel system, carbureted or fuel injected, has a throttle of some kind, a plate that opens as you step on the pedal. (Most people don't know it, but when you're "stepping on the gas" you're really stepping on the air pedal; that is, letting more air in, which pulls more gas in with it.)

In fuel-injected cars, when you "step on the gas," you're moving the throttle plate, which is allowing more air to come in. And as more air flows in, all these different sensors are on the alert and reading all this information about the air speed, the barometric pressure, the throttle position. All this information goes to the computer, which tells the injectors, "Okay, send in more clowns." That is, gasoline.

In the case of a *throttle body fuel-injection system,* one injector (or in some larger engines, two) sits right on top of this throttle body (which actually looks a lot like a carburetor). It squirts the gasoline into the airstream instead of directly into the cylinders. If you take the air cleaner off and run the engine, which you can do, you can actually see the fuel squirting down right on top of the throttle plate. It's kind of cute. And it's nice, because you can tell if the thing's working.

The most precise fuel-injection system is the *multipoint,* which is sequential; that is, fuel injectors get a pulse and fire a charge of fuel exactly when that cylinder needs it. It's more expensive than the throttle body because it has as many injectors as you have cylinders. The least expensive is the throttle body.

The truth is—and most people find this out rather painfully—if you have a late-model car that has a carburetor, one of those feedback carburetors (not feedbag, feedback!), you're in for a shock if you ever have to get it replaced. Those carburetors cost upward of a thousand bucks! That's $1,000, a one and three zeroes, no kidding.

It's amazing how many people think that carburetors still cost $150. And they have their mechanic replace it and then find out with the tax and the labor and gratuity and all that that the bill's $1,500! It's a rude awakening.

A fuel-injected car, on the other hand, has some expensive components, but they're all separate. I mean, you might have a $250 fuel pump and injectors that cost $50 apiece. But the likelihood of everything going at once and costing you a fortune is pretty small. Whereas if the carburetor on your late-model car conks out and you can't find any unemployed NASA engineers that are willing and able to rebuild it, then you're gonna be stuck for a brand-new one.

You should never have to replace *all* of the components in your fuel-injection system. When the boys at the shop tell you you need everything, tell them they need another sucker.

So let's talk about what *does* go wrong. People are afraid of fuel-injected cars because they figure when something goes wrong, they'll never figure it out themselves. And that's true. The same is true with your ignition system these days. It's all electronic and all computer controlled, and you're not gonna figure out what's wrong with it either.

But in nine cases out of ten, when a car won't run and it's either not getting fuel or it's not getting a spark, it's usually something simple. It's a broken wire or you're out of gas. You're not getting gas up to the injectors because there's no gas in the tank or the fuel-pump fuse is blown or the relay is no good.

So you should know where your fuses are, not just for your fuel-injection system, but for your windshield wipers, your heater fan, for everything. You don't want to have to locate them some night during a snowstorm, or worse than that, on the way to your wedding. Unless you need a good excuse for not showing up.

* * *

The number-one enemy of any fuel system is dirt. (Remember *Bonnie and Clyde*? "Dirt.") Dirt usually comes in the form of rust, and it can either be made or borrowed.

You can "borrow" dirt from the fuel tank of the guy you're buying the gas from. You have a little fifteen- or twenty-gallon tank in your car, and you're buying gasoline from a station that has a giant underground tank, in most cases made out of metal and in many cases older than your uncle Fred's dog.

The tank rusts. And that rust gets mixed in with your gasoline, or his gasoline, and he sells you the rust along with the gasoline. Or he throws it in free.

Of course, your gasoline tank in most cases is also made out of metal, so on a smaller scale you're also manufacturing rust, especially if you're a cheapskate and keep the gas gauge down around "E" all the time. The condensation that forms inside the almost-empty tank is creating rust, and that rust mixes with the fuel and eventually plugs up your injectors.

The best way to safeguard against this is to change the fuel filter regularly. It's amazing how many people never change their fuel filter until the car stops running. Again, you think, "Oh, boy, the worst has happened," and all you really need is a filter.

Fuel filters aren't cheap. So when you go into one of these cheapo places for a $29.95 tune-up, it's unlikely that they're changing a $32 gas filter as part of the job. Bear that in mind, and remember Click and Clack's Adage Number One: *It's the Stingy Person Who Spends the Most.*

Eventually that fuel filter will get plugged up. If you're lucky, the car will stop. If you're not, it'll keep running long enough to plug up your injectors and do some real damage. So it's important to change the fuel filter once a year. I don't care what the book says. Change it once a year and you'll avoid a lot of misery.

* * *

We ought to mention vapor lock.

Gasoline boils at something like 110 degrees Fahrenheit. So if it gets really hot under the hood and the pressure in the fuel line isn't high enough to keep the gasoline as a liquid—for example, when you turn the car off—it'll become vapor and just sit there in the fuel line and sometimes the car won't start. We say it's "vapor locked" because this hunk of vapor is exerting pressure and keeping the gas from flowing.

There's not much you can do about this, except to avoid traffic jams on hot days. If you have vapor lock, open the hood, let the thing cool off, and have a good book on hand to read all the time! It might be a good time, in fact, to read your owner's manual. You can brush up on all the things you should've been doing to your car for the last 25,000 miles.

There's a lot of confusion about pinging and knocking and octane ratings. If we ever figure it out, we'll let you know. But seriously, pinging and knocking are just two versions of the same thing. A ping is a less severe form of a knock. Both are caused by improper combustion taking place inside the engine.

The gasoline is supposed to burn very smoothly, and only when the spark plug ignites it. But if the gasoline gets too hot, or if it has too low an ignition temperature, it can be ignited by hot spots in the combustion chamber; then it begins to burn in various places all at once. These walls of flame collide, and the sound you hear is the knock or ping inside the engine.

This not only robs power, it's also bad for the engine, because the places where these walls of burning gasoline collide are very hot. And if they're always occurring at the same spot, they can burn valves or even burn holes in the pistons.

Not a nice thought, especially if you're a piston.

So engine knock is to be avoided. One of the things that causes knocking is excessive engine operating temperature. A car that ordinarily doesn't knock may develop a ping on a day when it's a hundred degrees. That's okay if it doesn't happen all the time; you can live with a little occasional knocking.

If you're in the wrong gear all the time, if you forget to downshift so you're in fourth gear when you really should be in third, you're also gonna get knocking. This is called "lugging" the engine, and you can avoid it by shifting down.

But the main thing that causes knocking is fuel that's the wrong octane rating. The higher the octane number, the more the gasoline costs and the more slowly and smoothly it burns; that is, the more it will prevent pinging and knocking.

So if you have a car that pings even after a tune-up, and your mechanic can't adjust the timing to get rid of it, and the EGR* system is working correctly, and all the little things that could cause it to knock have been examined, then you might try using a slightly higher-octane gas.

But if the car doesn't ping on the cheap stuff, use the cheap stuff. Using gas which is *too high* in octane wastes money and pollutes the environment more.

One final thing we haven't discussed is fuel-system ventilation. Because there isn't any.

Fuel systems are sealed now, so gasoline vapors cannot escape into the atmosphere. Most cars use a charcoal canister to trap the vapors, and hold them until they eventually get sucked into the engine and burned. If you miss the good old days, you can break open the canister and smell the charcoal.

The parting words are: dirt hurts. Change the fuel filter, because that's the *one* thing you really have to do to maintain the fuel-injection system. Other than that, it's pretty maintenance-free, believe it or not.

I think the biggest advantage of fuel injection, aside

*Exhaust gas recirculation. See why we didn't spell it out?

from the fact that it's more efficient and it helps to keep the atmosphere clean, is that as mechanics get more and more familiar with it, they'll realize that it's actually simpler to diagnose than carburetors.

A carburetor has so many pieces inside that you can't see. And in order to find out what's really going wrong with the carburetor, especially the hairy ones (And, oh, man, there are pieces in there!), you have to take it apart. And even after you take it apart, you still can't figure out what's wrong. And, worse than that, you can't figure out how to put it back together!

The advantage of fuel-injection systems is that they are made in discrete subsystems, or pieces. Mechanics can test each piece. We can put a voltmeter across terminal 3 and terminal 7 and determine that there's something wrong with the air-mass meter. Or we can determine that the temperature sensor has the wrong resistance, and for thirty bucks we'll put a new one in there and try it out.

All these things add up to fuel injection being the way to go. Don't be afraid to buy a fuel-injected car, because fuel injection's where it's at.

Trust us on this. (You have no choice, anyway. The carburetor is going the way of the dinosaur.)

And change that filter.

Fuel Pressure

CLICK: Hello, you're on *Car Talk*.

I have a question about a 1984 Saab. First, I'd like to corroborate your feelings about Saab radios. Mine lasted a week. I even had a sign in my window saying No Radio.

CLICK: You lied!

CLACK: I have a sign in the window of my old Chevy that says *Valuable 8-track Tape Player Inside*. But I can't find any takers.

CLICK: You know, it's a pretty sad state of affairs if you have a nice car like a Saab or a BMW and you have to ride around without a radio.

Yeah, true. At any rate, my problem is that the car runs great cold, but sometimes—not always—when it's warm, it will suddenly start losing power. The idle speed drops and becomes irregular. It stalls at lights, has poor acceleration, misses. Next day it runs great again. Maybe three days later the problem shows up again.

CLACK: So sometimes when it's warm it runs well.

Sometimes when it's warm it runs excellently. Sometimes when it's warm it chokes and sputters and the idle gets very irregular.

CLICK: This car's fuel injected.

Right.

CLICK: And there are certainly a lot of things it could be.

Well, let me tell you what it isn't. I've checked almost everything I can think of. It's got new plugs, new wires, new rotor, cap, fuel filter, the line pressure's okay, the control pressure's okay. . . .

CLACK: You had the control pressure checked when it was running well?

That's right.

CLACK: That doesn't tell you anything. You need to check it when it's not running well.

Well, but it tells me that the warm-up regulator, for example, at least works some of the time, right?

CLICK: That's what my guess is: that it works some of the time.

I don't understand how one of those could sometimes work and sometimes not work.

CLACK: I don't know either, to tell you the truth, but we've seen many cases where that occurs. And especially when the thing gets hot, it'll go cuckoo.

This warm-up regulator, it operates only when it's warm, right?

CLICK: It operates all the time. As the engine warms up, the pressure keeps going up and up and up; it constantly increases the pressure on the fuel distributor and lets less and less fuel in as the engine warms up. So basically, it's acting as a choke would on a carbureted car.

CLACK: But it could go cuckoo, and the pressure would start dropping instead, as the engine warms up, flooding everything. Ordinarily, ignition problems will manifest themselves as a high-speed miss. They'd be less apt to act up at low speed. In fact, you can take a car that's got very poor spark, and almost always it will idle correctly, because the spark is not asked to do very much. At high revs, when there's a lot of turbulence in the cylinders, a weak spark cannot jump the electrodes and you develop a miss. Your problem is low speed, not high. So, my guess is that your problem is not electrical, but rather a fuel problem.

Okay.

CLICK: It could also be you have an erratic fuel pump, which is something more apt to misbehave hot. So that's another thing to have your mechanic check when the engine's hot.

Should I just replace both of those things and hope it fixes the problem?

CLICK: You're looking at $300.

CLACK: You'd be hard pressed to buy a control-pressure regulator for less than $125 for that car, and the same is probably true of the fuel pump. So you're looking at a few bucks. My guess is that one of those two, or both of them, is the problem, and chances are that if you replace them, you're gonna solve it. But you'd be awfully upset with me if that didn't do it.

Right, I would.

CLICK: What I recommend is that you take it into a shop and have them run it for three hours. If that fuel pump is gonna malfunction, it'll malfunction in that period of time, in all likelihood.

CLACK: Bring it in on the hottest possible day. The next time the weatherman says it's gonna be 95 degrees.

Okay, thanks a lot.

Jumping Volvo

CLICK: Hello, welcome to *Car Talk*.

Hi, I'm from Newton, Massachusetts.

CLACK: Hi, Newton. How are you?

I'm good, thanks. I've got a '77 Volvo, and the problem is that as long as I keep a full tank of gas in it, it's fine. But as soon as it gets less than like half a tank, it lurches and jumps and goes crazy, and nobody's been able to figure out why.

CLICK: Some Volvos have two fuel pumps. If I'm not mistaken, this car has what's called a prepump in the tank, and that might not be working. Or it might be that the pickup inside the tank is plugged up. That's even more likely. I assume you've had the typical stuff done, like a tune-up and all that jazz, and the fuel filter replaced?

Yeah, all of that.

CLACK: I think it's either the prepump or a plugged fuel pickup. Inside the tank there's a screen that is supposed to filter out gross-sized particles like rocks and whatever. It might be plugged up.

Why would it only do it when it's half full or less?

CLACK: Because the bottom half of the screen is plugged up and the top half isn't. It's sort of a long, skinny screen.

CLICK: At any rate, you'll have to have your mechanic take out the tank and clean it out, if nothing else. Because if it's plugged up it means there's a lot of junk in there.

CLACK: Your kids missing any sneakers or anything?

I'll check.

Pop Pop

Hello, Car Talk. I have a small Olds V-8 that starts beautifully, runs beautifully, but after it goes about two blocks or three blocks in cold weather, it pops through the carburetor, pop pop, and it sort of tries to stall. After about two minutes of driving, it gets better.

CLACK: I like that *"pop pop."* Can you do that again?

Pop pop.

CLICK: So it's not when you first start it, and it's not after it's warmed up, it's right in the middle.

Right.

CLICK: It may be that your choke's opening too fast. Either because it's set initially too lean, or the choke unloader or the vacuum breaker—the pulloff, some call it—is pulling off too quickly or too much. But improper timing could also cause that same problem. When a car is incorrectly timed, it shows it, generally through poor performance when the engine is cold. Once the engine is up to operating temperature, it's extremely forgiving. You can drive a car with the timing retarded ten degrees perfectly well after it's warmed up. It's getting through that first few minutes that can be aggravating.

CLACK: Right. And when you first start it, it doesn't exhibit these problems, because it's racing and you don't notice it. It's just when the choke starts to open that it's gonna exhibit rotten performance.

CLICK: So have the timing checked and the choke adjusted and I bet that'll fix it.

CLACK: Good luck.

A Ping

I have a question about gasoline, I think. I have a 318 Chrysler engine in a '78 Cordoba.

CLACK: With crushed Corinthian leather seats, yeah.

Well, at 60 or 65 miles per hour, it pings like a son of a gun. I use the best-octane gasoline, 91 or above, and I pay those extra few cents like you were talking about last week, just to eliminate that possibility. And I heard you talk about this problem a couple of weeks ago, that it could be somehow overheating, but my indicator doesn't show that. And you said it could be a vacuum leak somewhere, and then I heard, then you said it could be overadvanced timing or it could be the EGR. So I don't know what the heck it is—

CLICK: It pings at a steady 60 or 65, or only on acceleration?

It does ping a little bit on accleration, but it's most noticeable when you're going a steady 60, or even 55. You can hear it real bad.

CLICK: Well, it could be any of the things you mentioned. It could also be that the pistons are very badly carboned up from a lifetime of driving in the city, in which case you're never gonna fix that.

Well, I did buy this car used. It's a '78, as I told you, and I bought it about three months ago from a little old lady who drove it to the train station every day, and not much more, and it had only 36,500 miles on it three months ago. I've put 3,000 miles on it since then.

CLICK: Well, she probably did drive it at 20 miles per hour around the city. And that would certainly build up carbon.

So is my using the best gasoline helpful?

CLACK: Maybe a little. But that's all.

CLICK: I would check all the other things. Make sure it is not overheating. Make sure you do not have a vacuum leak, and that your EGR system is working. Then use the highest-octane gas you can, and keep driving it at 50 or

60. If you're lucky, you'll burn off the carbon before the pistons melt.

CLACK: Or if you don't want to wait that long, take off the heads and scrape down those pistons. That's a nice Sunday afternoon job.

Chevy El Camino

CLACK: Hello, you're on *Car Talk.*

Hi, I'm John, from Twig, Minnesota.

CLICK: Hi, John. What's happening in Twig?

I've got a '73 Chevy 350 El Camino.

CLACK: That's all that's happening in Twig? I thought you had to live in Texas to drive one of those.

Oh, Minnesota's got more pickups than Texas, any day. I live about twenty miles from Duluth. Duluth, you know, sits down on Lake Superior, and we're up over the hill about twenty miles away.

CLICK: Looking down on it.

Yeah. When I go into town, I go down the hill. And when I get ready to stop, the engine stops before the car does. And that leaves me without power steering.

CLACK: Or power brakes or anything.

It gets disconcerting.

CLICK: Does this ever happen when you're just driving on a straightaway?

No. Only when I coast down the hill and I get ready to stop, it quits.

CLACK: Only on a downhill?

Yeah, only on a downhill.

CLICK: Does the motor run really smooth if you're driving on a flat road?

Yeah.

CLICK: And if you stop at a light, for example, it doesn't shake a little bit? Tell the truth, now.

It doesn't shake. But it will stall once in a while at a stoplight.

CLACK: Aha! It's probably idling too low.

CLICK: Yeah, when you're coasting down the hill, it's idling and it stalls. It's the same at a stoplight, only it's not idling for as long a time.

Okay, here's another thing: It doesn't idle at the same speed all the time.

CLACK: Withholding evidence from us! You can't do that!

CLICK: That's good, that's good. The first thing that occurs to me, if it's not running smoothly and occasionally stalling, and it doesn't run at the same idle speed all the time, it sounds right away like a vacuum leak. It could be a hose, but it's probably your carburetor. The rod that runs through the carburetor and holds the throttle plates.

So I need a new carburetor?

CLICK: That would be my guess. The hole where the rod runs through is worn and it's leaking air.

That's what I figured, because I already changed everything else.

CLACK: You wasted your time calling us. You don't need us.

Well, the call was free.

The Swedish Meatball Light

CLICK: Hello, you're on *Car Talk*.

This is Bart, I'm calling from Owensboro, Kentucky. I'm thinking of buying this 1980 Volvo, okay?

CLICK: It's okay by me.

It's got about 60,000 miles on it, which is not so bad. But there's a light on the dashboard, a warning light that comes on.

CLICK: EXH, it says.

No, it's SOND.

CLACK: Oh, SOND, yes. That's Swedish for EXH.

I don't know what it means.

CLICK: It doesn't mean a thing! It gets tripped by the odometer, and it's telling you that the emission control system should be checked. On most cars it comes on every 30,000 miles.

Oh.

CLICK: Right. So at 60,000 miles the light comes on. It is reset by a secret switch under the dashboard.

CLACK: Known only to three Swedish mechanics.

CLICK: If you poke around under the dashboard, you might find the switch, if you're lucky. But what it's really asking you to do, or telling you to do, is to take the thing into the dealer and have the emissions system checked. Which you should in fact do.

I'm afraid they'll charge me about $400 just to turn the light off.

CLICK: Well, one of the things they'll probably do at 60,000 is change something called the oxygen sensor. And the oxygen sensor is about a hundred bucks. The oxygen sensor reads the amount of unused oxygen in the exhaust gas. Then it sends a signal to the computer, which then goes ahead and adjusts the mixture. It should be changed at 60,000 miles. We've seen Volvos that go over 100,000 miles and never have the thing changed. But they run real lousy.

They should replace that, huh?

CLACK: Yes. But it's not your car anyway, so what do you care?

Well, it will be if I decide to buy it.

CLICK: How did you hear about this car?

My preacher used to own it.

CLICK: Where did he get it fixed?

CLACK: He never got it fixed. That's why he's selling it.

No, it's in pretty good shape.

CLICK: 60,000 miles is early in the life of a Volvo. This thing could easily run for 200,000. Do you mind telling us how much he wants for this?

$4,000.

CLICK: And it's not rusted?

No, no rust. We don't use a lot of salt down here. Except on our hams.

CLACK: Hams?

High Mileage

CLICK: Hello, you're on the air.

I have a 1979 Volvo, and I have a question about it. The car has fairly high mileage.

CLICK: How high?

160,000 miles.

CLACK: Yeah, that's what I would call fairly high mileage, even for a Volvo.

I've had the car about five weeks, and when I bought it I knew it needed a tune-up, because I had it checked out before I paid any money for it.

CLACK: Yeah.

I took it in for the tune-up. They adjusted the valves and everything, and when they took it out and road tested it, the thing stalled every time that they came to a stop. So they took it back and they checked the fuel pressure, the pump volume, they cleaned out the flow plate, and the fuel sensor plate.

CLICK: In other words, everything having to do with the fuel injection.

And they thought it was okay. I went to pick it up and the thing started stalling the minute I backed it out of the lot. And it's continued ever since. I've taken it back to them once, and after another day of looking at it, they say it needs a control-pressure regulator.

CLICK: $150. So you did it.

No, I haven't done that yet. I said, "Is there any way of getting the thing to pass the emissions test?" because it was running perfectly before I took it in. No stalling or anything.

CLACK: Now it'll stall every time you sit at idle?

When it's cold, it idles well. But as soon as the car warms up—

CLICK: If it idles well when it's cold, it's an indication that the control-pressure regulator's working. If I had to guess, I'd say you need injectors.

CLACK: Gee, that's what I would guess.

Oh, really?

CLICK: That's a guess. Obviously. These guys may have a better guess, because they've been playing around with it for hours.

CLACK: Do they have any explanation for why it started stalling since they tuned it up?

They claim it's an intermittent problem with the control-pressure regulator.

CLICK: They're nuts. Isn't it curious that the car didn't have this problem before you brought it in to them?

CLACK: Yeah. Before they adjusted the valves. My guess is that they adjusted the valves too tight.

CLICK: Right. Ask them to readjust.

CLACK: And if that doesn't work, I'd check the injectors. They must have four injectors kicking around. Tell 'em to put some in and try it. They're easy to put in, it takes twenty minutes, and if they solve the problem, hallelujah! If they don't, they can take 'em out and put 'em back on the shelf. But I would certainly try that next.

CLICK: It's also possible that they have monkeyed around with the mixture, trying to get you to pass the emissions test, and that's why you're stalling. Now, if they turn that little three-millimeter Allen screw one way or the other, they'll make it flunk the test, but it'll probably run great, like before.

Okay.

CLICK: But if these injectors have been in there for 160,000 miles, which is very possible, you're ready for new ones.

They claim they can't set it and keep it at a particular setting for any length of time, that it wanders.

CLICK: That's funny, I had a Volvo just the other day, or a week or two ago. I mean, it was last year, I think. Sometime.

CLACK: The days all run together.

CLICK: Yeah. And it was doing exactly the same thing. Take your foot off the gas, it would cut out every time. I put four injectors in this thing, and jeez, it ran like a new car. If they want to try the control-pressure regulator, tell 'em to try it. But if it doesn't work, you want 'em to take it out. And tell 'em to try the injectors, if that doesn't work. And if they don't work, you'd like them to take those out too. And you can junk it. My brother will give you a hundred bucks for it, he's got the same car. Use it for parts.

CLACK: Or it'll make a good doghouse. You got a dog?

The Car Owner's Lament

This is Karen calling from Palo Alto, California, and actually my car problem has been solved.

CLACK: Let's talk about something else, then. How's the weather?

What I need now is advice on whether to keep the car or not. What I have is an '84 Mitsubishi and it just returned from five weeks in the shop. The thing wouldn't start, and I finally got it to someone who discovered that the valves had been burned and it needed a valve job. So he took the head off and did a valve job and the thing still wouldn't start.

CLICK: Sounds like a normal day in the auto business.

So then he checked the exhaust manifold and found a second catalytic converter there, and it was all plugged up. And as a result, all the exhaust gas that had to go out couldn't go out and went back in and just blew everything to pieces.

CLICK: That's why you probably didn't need the valve job in the first place.

What my mechanic said was that it's a really bad design to have two catalytic converters, especially having one inside the exhaust manifold. He thinks I should junk it and get a new car. I don't know what to do. So what do you guys think I should do?

CLACK: How much did you spend on this little operation?

About $1,200. It's been a real costly endeavor.

CLICK: Well, I can understand your feeling a little down on the car. But there are a lot—not a lot, but there are some cars that have two converters. That's not a problem in and of itself. The problem is, what led to the clogging of the converter? The engine running too rich can cause that, so there may be some fuel system problem. Your problem may not be over if they haven't found the cause of all this. That primary converter didn't get all clogged up for nothing. Something may have caused it. How many miles do you have on this thing?

75,000 miles.

CLACK: On the other hand, maybe nothing's wrong with the fuel system. Maybe it was just its time to have the converter replaced. They don't last forever.

CLICK: But if you decide to keep it, then you should get the whole fuel system checked out. If it passes the California smog test, then you're probably okay.

Actually, it did have a hard time passing its last smog test.

CLICK: That could've been because the converter wasn't working. Have it done again, and if it still has trouble passing, then something is wrong.

CLACK: And then sell it.

CLICK: The real question is, do you love it?

CLACK: No, she hates it!

I don't know. I love it and hate it at the same time.

CLICK: The car owner's lament.

8

THE CLICK & CLACK COMFORT/LUXURY/ CONVENIENCE TRADE-OFF MATRIX

Major Myths and Popular Delusions About Car-Buying Strategies

Take this little quiz.

TRUE OR FALSE

1. A car is just a way to get from here to there.　　　　　T　F

2. I have so much money that it doesn't matter how much I spend for a car.　　　　　T　F

3. I would like people to believe that I have so much money that it doesn't matter how much I spend for a car.　　　　　T　F

4. A car is a macho device for displaying power and venting frustrations.　　　　　T　F

MULTIPLE CHOICE

5. Which is greater: $600 or $3,600?
   A. $600 is greater
   B. $3,600 is greater
   C. Approximately the same
   D. Don't know

6. Given the choice, I'd rather spend my money on
   A. Myself
   B. My car
   C. Doesn't matter; my car and I are equal
   D. What are you talking about?

RESULTS:
If you answered 1F, 2T, 3T, 4T, 5C, and 6C, then you have just been accepted to Harvard. Any other combination of answers gets you into the Click and Clack Institute for Psychosocial Research (as a *patient,* not as a student!).

These few questions are cleverly designed to uncover your underlying motives for owning a car. If the psychology of your motives is too deep for us to penetrate, then this chapter is not for you. This chapter is about money and the car-buying strategies that can help you save money. But, at the same time, we recognize that the psyche is fragile, and we don't want to mess with yours. (Well, maybe just a little.)

Here's the situation. Some people use a car-buying strategy that costs them much more than it has to. If you're spending too much and you'd like to be helped, then this chapter can help—mostly by dispelling some of the common myths and misconceptions about the costs of owning a car.

But not everyone *wants* to be helped. For example, if your masculinity (or femininity) is all wrapped up in the kind of car you drive, then far be it from us to mess with that!

If you're on the borderline, then here's a little enticement to read on. Over the next twenty years, if you change your bad habits, you could have somewhere between $20,000 and $40,000 in the bank; or you could have spent it on *yourself* instead of on your car. (Maybe a few trips to Hawaii. Or a hair transplant. Or a fat farm. Whatever.)

Here are some of the myths and misconceptions that lead people down the wrong path.

MYTH NUMBER ONE: THE COST OF FIXING A CAR GOES UP AND UP AS THE CAR GETS OLDER AND OLDER.

Why do we think this? Well, if you have ever owned a new car, you will have noticed that during the first year, you spend practically nothing for repairs. Sure, you change the oil and have the 10,000-mile checkup, but nothing breaks. You spend maybe $100 on "maintenance." The second year, a few things wear out and maybe something even breaks. You fix it. The third year, even more things wear out and more things break. By the fourth year not only are new things wearing out but some of the things you repaired in the second year are worn out *again!* Hmmm, you say. This is running into money. In fact, if you made yourself a little plot of what you had spent, it might look like this:

Now, here's where you can get into trouble. You look at this diagram and you commit the unpardonable sin. You *extrapolate*. I mean, it's the natural thing to do. You see a few points and what else can you do? You have seen the future and it is this:

Ouch! you say. Not only is this running into money, it's going to run into even *more* money. It looks like in year six or seven the cost of keeping this dog on the road is going to approach the national debt.

Well, you're wrong. The curve does *not* continue to rise. After about the third or fourth year *it levels off!* It looks like this:

There have been lots of studies that PROVE that the costs level off. Government studies prove it. Hertz Corporation studies prove it. And the vast (or is it half vast?) experience of Click and Clack proves it. This is very significant. The costs of repairing a car level off at about $600 a year, on average. Of course, it's more for some cars, less for others; but the important thing is that *it levels off!* So, if you kept a car for a very long time, it would cost you—on average—about $600 a year to keep it *safely* running.

Compare this to the alternative of buying a new one. Payments to the bank for a relatively inexpensive new car are about $300 per month, or $3,600 a year. Question 5 of the quiz at the beginning of this chapter asked the tough question: "Which is greater: $600 or $3,600?" Please think carefully about the answer to this question. We'll be coming back to it later.

MYTH NUMBER TWO: DEPRECIATION IS KILLING ME. I'D BETTER SELL THIS HEAP NOW, WHILE IT'S STILL WORTH SOMETHING.

Oh, this is a beaut. This myth is especially dangerous, because it appears to have some significant economic or financial derivation; that is, it sounds like someone smart figured it out. Wrong again. It was not someone smart. It was an accountant! And in our never-ending search to overcome obfuscation and confusion, we, Click and Clack, will now dispel the Depreciation Myth. Here it is:

Depreciation is horsefeathers.

Depreciation only means something *when* you decide to trade in your car. But it doesn't mean *anything* if you decide *not* to trade in your car. So you can't use it to decide *if* you should trade in your car. This has been proven in the laboratory. It is a Great Unyielding Truth. Only a fool or a used-car salesman (is that redundant?) would try to use depreciation to decide *whether* to buy a new car.

So what do you use if you can't use depreciation? Right. Your head.

Here's a small hint to get you thinking in the right direction. Remember Question 5 in the quiz? "Which is greater: $600 or $3,600?" Isn't it really that simple? I mean, if you're trying to decide between two alternatives and one costs $600 and the other costs $3,600, does it take a brain surgeon or a rocket scientist to figure out which one's cheaper? Sure, you can make the question more complicated. Sure, you can confuse the issue. Sure, you can obfuscate the analysis. Sure you can. Are you an accountant?

But think about it. If you currently have a car that's paid for, then it will cost you, on average, $600 for upkeep next year. If you sell it and buy a new one, then depending on what you buy and how much yours is worth, it will cost something other than $600. Will it be less than $600? That is, will the payments to the bank be less than $50 per month? Dream on!

MYTH NUMBER THREE: NEVER BUY A USED CAR. YOU'RE ONLY BUYING SOMEONE ELSE'S TROUBLES. "

The trouble with old wives' tales is that they sound good. Just like this one sounds good. I mean, why would someone sell a car if it was a good car? The answer is in another great aphorism: "One man's trash is another man's treasure." People sell cars for lots of reasons. True, *one* of those reasons is that it's a lousy car. But that's not the *only* reason that people sell cars. Think about all the other possible reasons. Like:

Someone has another kid and the family doesn't fit in the old car anymore.

Two people get married and they both own a car, but they don't need two cars.

Someone has a midlife crisis and *must* have a sports car.   *Jerry Lee Lewis*

And a great reason for you: Someone actually *believes* the depreciation myth and is selling the car while "it still has trade-in value."

And better yet—someone has had a few problems with his car and has done the extrapolation and therefore believes that next year's repair bills will be astronomical.

In these last two cases, you could say that instead of buying someone else's troubles, you're actually taking advantage of someone else's stupidity. What's wrong with that? It's the American way.

People buy about sixteen million *used* cars every year. A lot of them are okay. Are they perfect? No. Are you? (This is like the joke about the bachelor who was looking for the perfect woman to marry. He found her, but unfortunately she was looking for the perfect man!)

The key to a smart car-buying strategy lies in buying a *good* used car and keeping it forever (or ten years, whichever comes first). Remember this: It *is* possible to buy a good, even a great, used car. Remember this too: you probably wouldn't know a great used car if you saw one. Worse yet, you wouldn't know a heap either.

You know why women are better car buyers than

men? Because they're not ashamed to admit that they don't know diddly about cars. But macho men—they're another story. After all, how can you be a real man if you don't use words like "double overhead cam" or "crank-shaft" or "red line"?

I mean, really.

Most men refuse to admit that they don't know. (Like if I ever get lost, my wife says, "Hey, here's a revolution-ary idea! Why don't we stop and _ask_ someone how to get there?" Never! I'll find it!)

If you don't know, you _have to ask someone who does know_. But this relates to the next myth—

MYTH NUMBER FOUR: THE DAMN CAR HAS SO MANY PIECES THAT ANYTHING COULD BREAK AT ANY TIME WITHOUT ANY WARNING.

I guess I used to believe this too. I guess we all believe it about things that we don't really understand. I still believe it about my house. Things in my house break unexpectedly all the time. Pipes leak, wires melt, stuff keeps falling off the ceiling. I mean, _anything_ could hap-pen.

But like all the other myths, it just ain't true. _A good mechanic who knows what to look for can tell you what is about to break!_

Even a not-so-good mechanic is better at this than you are. So, if you are going to find a good used car, you _must_ have it checked out by someone who knows more than you. You pay him (or her) $100 and you save yourself a ton of money and headaches. A few examples:

—a car can run "perfectly" well and a compression test will tell the mechanic that it needs a $500 valve job.

ring!

—a clutch that will be garbage in a month will seem to operate fine right now (that is, during your test drive).

—a car with a barely perceptible 'shimmy' could need $500 of front-end work.

—an exhaust system that purrs like a kitten could have been patched up with furnace cement. Cost: $200 to $500.

The list could go on and on. Things that a test drive or a cursory examination will never uncover. The worst case we ever ran into was a car that one of our customers fell in love with. At our insistence, he brought it in for us to check. (We don't usually strongarm our customers like this, but this guy was a certified flake.) The car was pretty. Nice paint job, clean, and ran pretty well. The bottom line: the price of the car was $6,000 and it needed almost $3,000 worth of "hidden" repairs—all things that were *almost okay*. Like a starter motor, a clutch, brakes, and front end. *almost - but not quite*

CAR-BUYING STRATEGIES AND THE TRADE-OFF MATRIX

So. It *is possible* to know what's wrong with a used car *before* you buy it. It is possible to fix those things (or better yet, have the *seller* fix them). Therefore, you *can* buy a decent used car. *Yeah, sure - good Luck !*

Should you? Yes. Because in the short run *and* in the long run, it's cheaper. It's a lot cheaper; and you get to spend the leftover money on yourself!

Our car-buying lives stretch over fifty years (from age twenty to age seventy, at least). And doing the wrong thing for fifty years adds up to a huge pile of money, like maybe $100,000 to $150,000! That is, the difference between a smart car-buying strategy and a not-so-smart strategy can mean a *difference* of more than $100,000 in your pocket (or under your mattress).

Car-buying Strategies

There are all kinds of car-buying strategies. They range from buying a new car every year to buying the "best" heap you can find for under five hundred bucks. The latter is *always* cheaper. Don't let anybody tell you any different! If you buy a new car every year, you will *always* be paying the bank at least $4,000 a year. Always! And even a heap will last a year. (And if it doesn't, you could buy *eight* $500 heaps for $4,000). So, this strategy is always cheaper—in dollars. Of course, if you add in the psychological costs of headaches, worry, the inconvenience of breaking down, the embarrassment of driving a heap, then it's a different story. The guy with the new car has much more comfort, luxury, convenience, and reliability than you do.

[handwritten: generally speaking]
[handwritten: ego threat]
[handwritten: posi[tive] self imag[e]]

You have *traded* these things for *money.*

[handwritten: other things]

So who needs headaches, worry, embarrassment? The problem is that we *all* at some point in our lives have owned the proverbial sled. And we remember in great detail all those headaches. And now that we have "arrived" we are willing to pay to avoid them. *[handwritten: and pay dearly.]*

[handwritten: Re acut[e]]

But we go too far the other way. The pain of those memories is so vivid that we'll pay anything to avoid them again.

But here's the great discovery that has been made in the Click and Clack Institute of Paranormal Psychology and Charm School: You *can* have your cake and eat it too!

[handwritten: How so?]

There are strategies that lie between the two extremes mentioned above, and they work. If you adopt one of these in-between strategies, you can not only pocket a pile of money but you can also avoid *most* if not all of the inconveniences. The motivation for seriously considering one of the in-between strategies lies in the comfort/luxury/convenience trade-off matrix. What the matrix shows is the *difference* in dollars between various car-buying strategies. Here are the assumptions on which it is based:

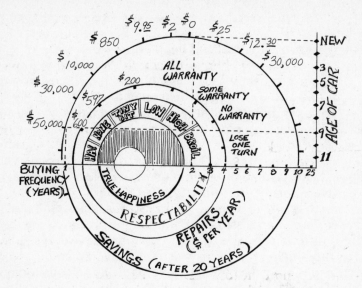

1. It is possible to buy a good used car.
2. It is possible to <u>know</u> <u>in advance</u> that something is going to break. *circa 1991 copy rite*
3. The average price of a new car is $12,000, and its price as it ages is the *Blue Book* price. *NAPA*
4. Any car will go 100,000 miles. (150,000 miles is also easy) but we'll be conservative and assume 100,000.
5. The average person drives around 10,000 miles a year; <u>a car should last ten years.</u> *plus*
6. Instead of a lifetime of buying cars, we'll be conservative and do the calculations for only twenty years.

To simplify the matrix, here are the strategies to be considered:

"A fool and his money.."

1. Buy a new car <u>every two</u> years.
2. Buy a three-year-old car and keep it for seven years. *"wisdom is better than gold and silver".*

" wise discretion shall sustain you.

3. Buy a seven-year-old car and keep it for three years.
4. Buy a nine-year-old heap every year.

All that NON-glitters is normally NON-gold

The matrix shows how much *more* it will cost you to adopt one of the strategies instead of another.

For example, the difference between Strategy 4 (buy a heap) and Strategy 1 (new car every two years) is fifty thousand dollars. That means you'll have fifty grand under your mattress at the end of twenty years, if you buy a heap instead of buying a new car every two years.

inflate

(Note for all the MBA types: Of course, $50K won't be worth $50K in twenty years. So you shouldn't put it under your mattress. But if you just put it into a savings account that paid the same interest as the average inflation rate during the twenty years, then you'd end up with a sum of money that will be as valuable as $50K is today.)

(Note for the accountants: Yes, this does not take taxes into account. So don't put the money into the bank; buy CDs. If you don't like CDs, buy tapes.)

So, you'll have the real purchasing power of $50K. That is, if $50K today will buy four years of tuition, then the amount of money you end up with in twenty years will also buy four years of tuition. If $50K will buy a Mercedes 300 today (it will), then you'll be able to buy one in twenty years with the money in the bank or invested in the CDs.

That's the biggest number in the matrix, but we don't necessarily recommend that everyone select Strategy 4. After all, we are talking about a *trade-off*, and in order to realize this much of a gain, you have to trade off an awful lot—mostly in the form of reliability, but also in the form of prestige. Most people's egos can't deal with what other people think about a person who's driving around in a nine-year-old rust bucket. (My car is *twenty-seven* years old; that tells you something about how much self-respect I have left. This is obviously the strategy for the real cheapskate.)

vanity

i.e., some prefer 'real frugalist'

Most people would probably opt for a little more respectability and reliability (They should go for Strategy 2 or 3. (My wife, after driving a thirteen-year-old Volvo, was tired of the snickers she got at the gas station and went for Strategy 2. A bit reckless, but she deserves it.)

Whatever you decide, remember that you're trading off comfort, luxury, convenience, reliability, and self-respect for money! Just to help you get through the hard times, here are a few ways to visualize the reward.

$50,000 = A two-week trip *every year* for twenty years to Hawaii (or Europe, or Hoboken, New Jersey) for you *and* your husband/wife or significant/insignificant other.

$50,000 = A wonderful intimate dinner for two twice a month in the fanciest restaurant you can think of (unless you live in Manhattan, in which case you wouldn't own a car and probably wouldn't be reading this book anyway. Why *are* you reading this book?).

$50,000 = One helluva payment on your mortgage.

$50,000 = A year off from work!

$50,000 = 5,000 anchovy pizzas. Think about this. 5,000 pizzas is ten pizzas a week for ten years; that's almost two a day EVERY DAY. You could eat pizza for ten years on the money you save on this strategy. A truly awesome thought.

Well, that's it: The Click and Clack Comfort/Luxury/Convenience Trade-off Matrix. Some have compared it to the general theory of relativity (but I'm too humble to believe it's that good.)

The Special Theory, maybe.

The Squeeze

CLACK: Hello, you're on *Car Talk*.

I'm from Stratford, Connecticut, my name's Mark. I have a slight dilemma. I'm a very tall person, and I need a fuel-efficient car for less than $10,000. And the only way I can shop for a foreign car is by sitting in a lot of them. And I've got a list of these things that is a mile long that I cannot fit into. But the ones I can fit into, I want to get your opinion as far as repairs.

CLICK: How tall are you?

I'm six-two. I have tried the Pontiac LeMans, the Ford Festiva, the Chevy Sprint. I'm nervous about the Sprint, because it's only a three-cylinder car— Shaker, Not Necessary a mover?

CLICK: You fit into the Sprint?

Shoe-horn
I can fit into it. It's tight.

CLICK: Yeah, but can you get out again?

CLACK: Who wants to get out? It's so much fun being in it.

Accord?

I tried the Hondas, the Subarus, but they're too small.

Civic?
CLICK: You say the Hondas are too small, but you can get into a Festiva?

Yeah.

CLACK: My refrigerator's bigger than the Festiva!

What can I tell you? I got more headroom there. I want to get your opinion on these three as far as a lot of stop-and-go city driving.

CLACK: The LeMans, the Festiva, and the Sprint? Look, you picked three dogs, if you want the truth.

Nite or AfterNoon

Sorry, that's all I've got to work with.

CLICK: Wait a minute! That can't be true. In the immortal words of former GM president Roger Smith, when asked by John White, who works for the *Boston Globe,* what kind of a car can an American buy if he wants to buy an American car for under ten grand and if he wants to buy a General Motors car? And Roger Smith thought for a second and said, "A two-year-old Buick." So you may want to buy yourself a secondhand larger car.

Yeah, but I'd like to keep with the fuel-efficient— ...

CLACK: Don't worry about the fuel efficiency. If you save enough on the car, you can afford to spend more on gas. Why are you so concerned with fuel efficiency? Do you drive many, many miles a year?

SAFari ? Suburban ?

Right now, I own a GMC van, and—

CLICK: Oh, I understand the whole psychology here. You're going too far in the other direction. The pendulum has swung.

CLACK: You're a little cuckoo right now, and you shouldn't make any important decisions. Years of getting 4 miles to the gallon can affect you like this. The fumes from inefficient combustion have obviously wiped out millions of brain cells.

CLICK: I had the same problem. I went the other way. I drove, for many years, an MGA, which is a car that not even mice can fit into. I got so sick of being crowded, that what did I do? I went out and bought a GMC Suburban. Biggest vehicle I could find. Because people go crazy. You go to the opposite extreme. There's no reason to go really crazy like that. Go to the middle.

CLACK: Yeah. How many miles a year do you drive?

Every day, about 60.

CLACK: That's <u>15,000 miles a year</u>. Buy a bigger car. If you drive that many miles, you don't want to drive it in a little, uncomfortable car. You'll be all cooped up in there. You'll go crazy. And you'll go buy another van.

CLICK: Go look at some larger cars and call us back next week.

CLACK: Either that(or buy the Sprint and take out the driver's seat. Sit in the back.) *seat*

I could do that.

innovate

CLACK: Yeah. Put some blocks on the pedals, you'll be all right. Thanks for calling, and good luck.

Click and Clack Decoder Ring

Hi, this is Ron, calling from Cincinnati. I'm a new listener to your show, and I get confused sometimes because I don't know when you guys are serious and when you're not. How can I tell when your answer to a call is serious?

CLICK: Evidently, Ron, you have not heard of the Click and Clack <u>Decoder Ring.</u>

CLACK: <u>Send us</u> $25 <u>in coin</u>—no worthless paper money, please—to WBUR, Boston, and you will get the Click and Clack Decoder Ring.

CLICK: You hang this up in front of your radio, and when it oscillates back and forth—

CLACK: It's not the kind of ring that you put on your finger, it's a piston ring!

CLICK: Right. You hang it from the rear-view mirror right over the dash, and it picks up the emanations from the radio. And when it begins to vibrate, it means we're lying. Or does it mean we're telling the truth? Which is it?

CLACK: I don't remember. It's in the instructions. I think.

A New Transmission Every Month

Hello, I'm Roger, from Los Angeles, the City of Angels, California. My question is this: I have a '79 Oldsmobile Cutlass with 98,000 miles on it, and I just changed the transmission in it, and I have a love-hate relationship with this car. What I want to know is, how do you know when to get rid of it?

RIPLEY ENTRANT

CLICK: When you go out in the morning (do you see vultures circling over the car?) Are the neighborhood cats trying to cover it up?

CLACK: Why would you want to get rid of this beauty?

Well, it seems like I'm always sinking money into it. Now it's the transmission. Next week it'll be the motor. I mean, it's got 98,000 now. I remember a gentleman called in last week about white smoke that comes out in the morning. Well, I get white smoke in the morning. I go through a quart of oil a month. I've gone through my third starter and my second—that thing for the brakes—master cylinder?

EXTRAPOLATION

white? (or blue)

CLACK: So what? If you're thinking about it purely from the standpoint of money—let's leave emotion out of it for the moment.

CLICK: Right. Let's leave out that Toyota Celica you've had your eye on.

No, I don't want a small car.

CLICK: What do you have your eye on, Rog? Come on. The truth.

I was thinking of the 190 Mercedes-Benz. Or maybe a DL Volvo, or something like that.

CLACK: Why were you thinking of these things? Do you think these thoughts in the presence of your '79 Cutlass?

I think those thoughts behind her back.

CLACK: From a purely economic standpoint, it never pays to get rid of your car. Never. So what if you put in a master cylinder? So what if you put in a transmission? « Does that come out to equal the bank payments » on this Mercedes that will require you to fork over $500 every month?

It'll be exactly that! And it's about $498 for the transmission.

CLICK: <u>Yeah</u>, but <u>that</u>'s <u>once</u>. Buying a new car is like putting in a new transmission *every month.*

I'm surprised that you said that. Because everybody else keeps telling me the opposite.

New car sales person
Bank loan officer
car insurance agent
teen-age children

CLACK: This is the only theory in the entire world of which I am sure. I don't know whether the earth goes around the sun or vice versa. I don't know about electromagnetism. But I do know that <u>it *never* pays to buy a new car.</u>

CLICK: He's right. It pays emotionally, spiritually, maybe; but economically, no. Most people <u>try to justify</u>

i.e., delude thems

buying a new car by using some economic rationale, but the truth is they're just afraid of a breakdown ⟨Fear is the great motivator.⟩

CLACK: And it's a good one. It keeps all those auto companies in business. And if you have to drive fifty miles a day, it's better to pay the bank than to worry yourself sick.

CLICK: Right. Bypass surgery costs more than a Mercedes.

Guts (Great Unyielding Truths)

CLACK: Hello, you're on *Car Talk.*

Hi. This is Janet from Nashville, and I have been listening to your show for years, and I agree with you about keeping your old car.

CLICK: ⟨We⟩ don't want to keep *our* old car. [We want ⟨you⟩ to keep *your* old car.]

intermediate

Well, that's what I've done. I have a 1977 Malibu and it's running great, but I have this problem. ~~ A.K.A. Buick century

CLACK: Which is . . .

It looks terrible. Every time I see somebody in a new car I get this terrible urge to buy one. Why, those undeserving z$!(·)² ̧x

CLICK: We can help you! We have a plan. You must have one of those franchises out there, where they paint cars. They're all over the place. Bake-on
Trust us to Bring Home the Bac-on

You mean, "Four million cars painted"—that kind of thing?

CLACK: Yeah. Most of them twice.

CLICK: No, they do a great job. <u>For the money,</u> it's the best paint job you're gonna get. You can get the Supremo Number One for $300 or something like that.

CLACK: You're just trying to freshen things up a bit. You don't want to drive an ugly car, right?

What if it were a GreMLiN, Pacer, Edsel, HeNrY J, PINTO, (etc.)?

I'm tired of it.

CLICK: You don't want the neighbors to know what a deadbeat you are! If you want to save some money, you can prep the thing yourself. You know, clean it up, make sure you wash it, sand it down, get it all good and cleaned, and let them do the painting.

CLACK: Yeah, and roll up the windows before you take it in; they might forget that. No, they do a nice job, those places. It's not going to be showroom. It's not gonna shine like it just rolled out of the factory. But for a car that's almost fifteen years old, it's going to look dandy!

1977
15
1992
(1991)

The vinyl roof looks terrible. Can that be painted?

CLICK: For $150 you could have a new vinyl top put on. Go for it.

CLACK: Or do what this friend of ours did. He covered the entire top of the car with Elmer's glue, and then sprinkled it with beach sand. A very unique look—

CLICK: On hot days he could sit up there and sunbathe.

CLACK: Except that it added considerably to the weight of the car. He had four flat tires the next morning.

So you really think it's worth keeping this old car?

CLICK: It depends on what you want. If what you want is a new car, nothing else will do. If what you need is maximum reliability, then buy a new car.

CLACK: On the other hand, think about what you'll do with the thousands of dollars you'll have saved after a few years.

CLICK: Think about all those vacations. Remember the fourteenth Click and Clack Great Unyielding Truth: "Memories are the only paradise from which man cannot be driven." Goethe helped us with this one.

CLACK: Seriously, it's worth keeping your old car if you think it would be really nice in fifteen years to have—let's see, ten trips to Waikiki, right? Or the down payment on a house. Or twenty-five pizzas.

CLICK: Twenty-five pizzas?

CLACK: We're talking serious pizzas here. $1,200 pizzas. Take-outs from Trump Pizza.

9

MAKING IT LAST

Tom: Well, we've managed to avoid this throughout the entire book, but here at the last chapter we find it necessary finally to identify ourselves. Here's why: If you've ever heard our radio show, you've probably noticed that we frequently don't agree. I mean, he's my brother and I love him, but sometimes his head just isn't screwed on right.

Ray: Yeah, sure. The reason we don't agree is that you're usually wrong about everything, and I am forced to be the voice of reason.

Tom: See what I mean? His head just isn't screwed on right. Anyway, this, the last chapter, is the one in which we disagree the most. My brother thinks that he's right because he thinks my position is based on my being a devout cheapskate, which seriously warps my perceptions and evaluations.

Ray: True.

Tom: The basis of our disagreement is that my brother thinks it's a good idea to buy a new car and I don't. I don't think he disagrees with everything regarding this chapter. Mostly he agrees, I think, with the underlying premises; he just thinks I go too far, that I'm too radical in my fanaticism about saving money. He thinks there are more important considerations than just saving money. He's right, of course, but he's also wrong. The reason that I'm so fanatical about saving money is this: If you spend more money, you have to earn more money; that means that you have to work more. But there are more important things in life than working. So, if you're a cheapskate, you can work less. *N'est-ce pas?* So, he's right, there are more important things than money. But that's why you should spend less. So you can have some time for the more important things.

Anyway, here's what we're gonna do. I (the handsome, intelligent older brother) will write the chapter as I think it should be written. And whenever my idiotic kid brother disagrees, we'll include his dissenting opinion. Okay? Here goes.

Ray (First dissenting opinion): It's obvious to anyone with any brains that it's my brother who has his head in the clouds. Also, it's pretty much agreed by anyone who knows us that I am the handsome, intelligent brother, and he is the dipstick of the family.

THE CHAPTER BEGINS HERE

If the last chapter convinced you that you should go for the $50,000 brass ring, then the question becomes "How to do it?" That is, how can you get a car to last forever? It boils down to this:

1. Buy the right car.
2. Maintain it.
3. Treat it gently; don't be a roughneck.
4. Fix things before they break.
5. Fix *everything* that breaks.
6. Don't give up when the goin' gets tough.

Ray: You dummy! If you're going to keep the car forever, doesn't it make sense to start with a new one?

Tom: Maybe; but let me continue.

Buying the Right Car

There are two aspects to this.

A) Buy one that is *mechanically* good.
B) Buy one that is *psychologically* good.

In the last chapter, we discussed the fact that *you* can't determine whether or not a car is mechanically good. Sure, you can check the *Consumer Reports* Frequency of Repair charts to make sure you're not getting a real lemon—and you *should* do that. But remember, the Frequency of Repair charts are *averages*. They have nothing to do with the *specific* car that you might buy. You must get a real professional opinion from a good mechanic. Otherwise you're shooting craps, and you'll probably lose.

Ray (Dissenting opinion): Wait a minute! This still assumes that everyone is going to buy a used car. Not everyone should buy a used car. There are lots of reasons why you should buy a new car. For example, how else can you take advantage of all the technological advances that take place from year to year? Like antilock braking systems (ABS) or air bags. If you have a ten-year-old car, you're always way behind and driving last year's technology. Or last decade's.

Tom (Rebuttal): Bull! First of all, there aren't that many advances. Sure, ABS and air bags are two, but how many more can you name? And if you buy a three- to five-year-old car, you can still get them anyway. Don't forget that the last chapter described this strategy as a *trade-off*, and that's exactly what you're doing—trading off certain things for money. Everyone has to decide the details of the trade-off for him/her self. If you can't live without ABS, fine. Almost every car on the road does *not* have ABS and we're all living without it. But I do agree that there will be some technical advances that the cheapskate doesn't avail himself of. Tough, but that's what trade-off means.

Ray (Rebuttal to the rebuttal): But the biggest trade-off you're making is in reliability. Heaps break down and new cars don't! Also, there are two other things that you *won't* get in a used car.

1. The new-car smell. Every laboratory in the world has attempted to capture this elusive essence, and no one has done it yet. Don't underestimate the psychological power of the new-car smell!
2. Cup holders. This is one of the major technological advances of the decade, culminating in the introduction of the Chevy APV, which has 14, count 'em, 14! cup holders. (Which is interesting, since it holds only six passengers. That's 2.333 cup holders per passenger. And they say the Japanese are ahead of us technically! Horsefeathers!)

Tom (Rebuttal to the rebuttal to the rebuttal): Sure, sure. My only answer to all this is the sign that hangs in Nissenbaum's junkyard: *What's wrong with used parts? All the parts in your car are used parts.* It's true that the older they get the more likely it is that they'll break, but that's why you have to read the rest of the chapter.

Ray: Okay, okay.

THE CHAPTER CONTINUES

"Psychologically good" is another issue. If you need a mechanic to help you decide if it's mechanically good, then you must need a shrink to help decide if it's psychologically good. And here I am: Dr. Clack.

Based on everything you've learned thus far from this book, you could probably figure this out for yourself. But for those of you who'd rather read than think, here goes:

What does it mean—"psychologically good"? It means a car that will not only please you now, but will even make you happy for many years. After all, the basis of the car-buying strategies is that you keep the car for a *long* time. If you don't like it to begin with, you're not going to like it *better* in five years. So the guiding principle when selecting the kind of car to buy should be this:

Don't Be Cheap. It's the Stingy (Wo)man Who Spends the Most.

When you're buying the car, it is not the time to save money. The underlying strategy will save the money for you later on.

What you have to remember when you're picking the car to buy is this: The reasons that cars don't last forever are not just mechanical reasons. The psychological reasons are just as important.

As an example, consider this. You're looking for a three-year-old used car. You find two that are acceptable; one has air-conditioning and the other doesn't. The one without is $500 cheaper. You cheap out. Next summer you're sweating while your deadbeat brother-in-law is driving around in air-conditioned comfort.

"That sleazeball! Is he better than me?" you say to yourself. "Don't I deserve A/C more than he does? Sure I do. I'm gonna sell this heap and get a nice new car *with* air-conditioning. And while I'm at it, I'm going for the leather seats and the power windows! I deserve it!"

There you are. Not mechanical failure. Psychological failure!

The rule is: Get everything you want—and more! Get all those options you always wanted, even the stupid frivolous ones. Live it up! Because not only do cars depreciate—so do the options! *Everything* is cheaper, so buy a car that you can *love!* Don't cheap out and give yourself an excuse next year to abandon your strategy and go out and spend $15,000 for a new car.

No excuses. Buy the car you love. Can you love a Yugo? For ten years? Get serious.

Ray: I don't have a serious problem with all this drivel, but I do want to add the voice of reason here. Do you really have to be married to the damn car? I mean really. Also, remember that what really makes you love a car is that it *runs!* You can be surrounded with crushed Corinthian leather, but if it breaks down three days in a row you'll hate the car *and* you'll hate all Corinthians too! (Where the hell *is* Corinthia, anyway?)

THE CHAPTER CONTINUES

So, first you fall in love with it, and then you find out what's wrong with it. You take it to your mechanic and ask him to check *everything* and give you an itemized list of all necessary and imminent (six to twelve months) repairs, with a cost estimate for each. Then you use this list to:

—get the seller to fix things, if it's a dealer;
—get the price down;
—or both.

If he no fix, you no buy. So what that you were in love for half a day? There are plenty of fish in the sea. (There are actually about 16,000,000 of them; that many *used* cars are sold every year. You'll fall in love again.) So,

1. Find the one that's psychologically right;
2. Check it out;
3. Get the list of repairs.

And Fix *Everything. Immediately!*

You must fix everything immediately, so that you'll be driving a "perfect" car right away. This means that you have to factor the costs of the repairs into your budget. If you have only $4000 to spend, you can't buy a $4,000 car that needs $1,000 of repairs. If you do, you won't do the repairs. If you don't do the repairs, none of this will work. The car will break down, you'll get ticked off, and before you can say "fender face" you'll be in the showroom plunking down $15,000.

Ray: If you *are* buying a used car, I agree that this is the way to buy it. But I think it should be a reasonable used car, not a heap. And don't forget the amount of time it takes to follow this strategy. My brother suffers from Unemployment Syndrome. You'd have to be unemployed to have enough time to do all this. Don't forget that you may have to look at two, three, or four cars to find the right one. Is your boss going to understand your taking all these days off? If you're self-employed, do you factor in all the money you will have lost during your search?

Tom: True. True. But if you're on unemployment, they don't care what you do every day. And you have to keep busy, don't you?

THE CHAPTER CONTINUES

Maintenance I

This is one of those things that's easy to understand and accept, but hard to do. Like—you know you shouldn't eat all that junk food and you promise yourself you'll quit. Until you pass that Burger King with the odor of fat dripping off the grill and you're done for. . . .

Maintenance is like that.

The owner's manual tells you everything that has to be done and when to do it.

So do it.

When it comes time for the 20,000-mile and 40,000-mile checkups, the car will hopefully be running great. So, there will be a tremendous temptation to forget about the checkup. You might even look in your bible of Great Unyielding Truths and come up with this one: *If it ain't broke, don't fix it.*

This is *not* a Great Unyielding Truth. Maybe it ain't broke now, but it will be broke soon. Things *do* wear out. Here's the *real* Great Unyielding Truth: *Do you want to drive it to get it fixed, or do you want to have it towed in at three A.M. from the dark country road in front of the Bates Motel?*

Do everything the owner's manual says.

The only departure from the owner's manual that we suggest is to change the oil every 3,000 miles, rather than the 7,500 or 10,000 that many manuals recommend.

From my vast (and my brother's half-vast) experience, the engines that keep on running forever are the ones in which the oil has been changed religiously (i.e., every Sunday if you're a Christian, Saturday if you're Jewish, and Tuesday at 3 P.M. if you're a follower of L. Ron Hubbard). Changing the oil gets rid of the dirt and sludge that collects in the oil. The only way to get rid of the dirt is to change the oil.

Change the Oil and Filter Every 3,000 Miles and Your Motoring Days Will Be Filled with Smiles.

Let It Go to 8 or 10K and You Will Live to Rue the Day.

Ray: My brother's bad poetry notwithstanding, I agree with all of this.

Maintenance II

Even with all the scheduled maintenance, things can still sneak up on you. So just to add a little insurance for your happy, carefree motoring, it's a good idea periodically to check out the entire car just like you did before you bought it. Take it to the mechanic and *make believe* that it's a used car you're thinking of buying. Have him go all through it and make the list of all things that are now wrong or are imminently going to go wrong.

Fix them.

We think that once every two years is about right for

doing this, but you could do it every year if you are especially paranoid. (It's not bad to be paranoid. For example, if you're a female who drives at night on lonely country roads, it's *good* to be paranoid.)

Ray: This is okay, but the truth is that some failures can't be predicted. Sure, the mechanic will find a hose or a belt that's about to break, but he may not know that your alternator is going to break before the next checkup. And if it does, you could well break down somewhere unexpectedly. The older the car, the more such things there are, and therefore the higher the likelihood that you'll break down. That's the strongest argument for buying a new car.

Tom: True. But the only real insurance against this is to have a new car all the time. What are you going to do? Buy a new car every six months? Even a two-year-old car will have unexpected failures. Hell, you can't protect yourself against everything! If you're that paranoid, you'd better just stay home.

THE CHAPTER CONTINUES

Driving Habits

1. Take It Easy

Ever see two cars which were once identical, except that now one is a heap and the other looks and drives like new? One might ask, "Why is that?" The answer is, "The owners." Owners wreck cars, mostly by being ruffians. Even more important than maintenance, treating the car *gently* is what keeps it from getting wrecked. Do *everything* gently. Don't jam the shifter into gear; slide it in gently. Don't whack the directional signal lever up and down; move it gently.

You don't have to prove that you're stronger than all those little knobs and switches. *You are.* They're just innocent, weak little devices. Be nice to them!

2. Start It Up Slowly

When you first start an engine that's been sitting in your driveway all night, all the oil has sunk to the bottom of the engine. It's had all night for gravity to pull it down. Unfortunately, all the parts of the engine that need lubrication are not down there at the bottom of the engine; in fact, they're all up higher. In fact, the only thing down there is the oil pump, the device that pumps the oil up to where it's needed. But the oil pump doesn't start working until the engine is turning. So those first few seconds after the engine starts are crucial to prolonging the life of the engine.

The absolute worst thing you can do is rev the engine the moment it starts.

Again, we all remember the days when we had cars that would barely start.

Ray: Some of us still do, bro.

Tom: So, the moment it "catches," there's an irresistible tendency to want to make sure it keeps running. So you floor it.

Vrrrrooooooooommmmmm. "There. It's running. Thank God."

Of course, this 'tendency' is even stronger on those dark, cold mornings in the northern half of the United States.

And, of course, that's the absolutely worst time to do it. The oil is like molasses when it's cold, and it's even harder to pump it up into the moving parts of the engine where it is needed.

Starting Instructions:
Turn the key.
Keep those size tens away from the gas pedal.
If it starts and then stalls, that's great.
Try again.
Have faith. It will start.

If it doesn't start, it's probably because you postponed a scheduled maintenance visit. Shame on you.

Some people worry that they'll kill the battery. You probably won't. Modern batteries are terrific. And so what if you do kill the battery? A battery costs sixty bucks; an engine costs $3,844.79. *plus TAX*

Ray: The jerk is right about this.

Warm it up?
No. Don't warm it up. The engine doesn't want to sit there doing nothing. [If it's running, you're ready to go.]! So go.
What you *do* need to do is to go slowly for the first three to five minutes on a really cold day. If you live one minute from the freeway, do not start it up and then go screaming down the road at 60 m.p.h. During those first few minutes, don't exceed 20–30 m.p.h. And don't do it in low gear, because that will make the engine rev too high (turn too fast). If you have a tachometer, keep it under 2,000–2,500 rpm. *or Vac. gauge needle above 10" Hg*

After five minutes, do whatever you want.

Got it?
Those first few seconds are crucial. *Don't rev it.*
Once it's running, drive. But drive slowly.
Seriously. This works.

Ray: He's right.

3. Other Driving Tips

Here are two ways to back out of a driveway.

A. —Put car into reverse.
   —Step on gas.
   —When car is out in the street, put car into drive.
   —Step on the gas.
B. —Put car into reverse.
   —Step on gas.
   —When car is out in the street, step on the brake.

—When car has come to a complete stop, put into drive.
—Step on the gas.

Notice that extra part in "B"—stepping on the brake? Almost seems unnecessary, doesn't it? I mean, why bother. The procedure in "A" accomplishes the same thing, doesn't it?

Yes, it not only accomplishes the same thing, but also accomplishes the gradual destruction of all the major pieces of the drivetrain. Think about what's happening. Everything is moving clockwise. Then you throw it into drive (or first gear, if it's a manual transmission). Suddenly, all those pieces that were moving clockwise are being asked to move counterclockwise.

Wham! What a cruel thing to do. Worse than cruel, it's expensive. To be specific:

It will wreck the constant velocity (C-V) joints.
They cost $200 to replace.
There are four of them.
And only one of you.
Don't do it.

Shakes and Rattles

The reason some cars have a million rattles is that they are literally shaking themselves apart. This happens partly from the way you drive and partly from the Click and Clack Law of Incrementalism. Here's what happens: You hit a bump or pothole, or you whack the curb when you're trying to park. You forget about it. And why shouldn't you? These things happen. And it doesn't seem to have caused any damage. The car feels okay.

But it's not okay. It's almost okay, but it's not okay.

(Whacking a curb will never make a car better than it was prior to hitting the curb) If you're lucky, it will make the car much worse. You'll be lucky, because it will be bad enough for you to *notice* that something happened.

Usually, though, you'll be unlucky, because the whack will not do enough damage to be noticeable. So you'll forget it. You'll develop a barely perceptible shake. Not enough to worry about. In fact, you'll get used to it. You won't even notice it.

Then it will happen again—another pothole or curbstone.

And the shimmy will get just a little worse. Incrementally worse. And here's where the Law of Incrementalism comes in. At no time is the shimmy or shake very much worse than it was before. So you never notice these very slight changes in the handling of the car, because the changes are—what?

Right. Very slight.

Incremental.

But they add up.

Have you ever driven down the highway and looked at the front wheel of the car next to you? The wheels on one car out of three are bouncing up and down like crazy. This is not good.

You might wonder "How can s/he drive like that? Isn't the damn steering wheel shaking out of her/his hands?"

Sure it is.

Does s/he notice it? Probably not, because it happened a little bit at a time.

The same thing happens with noises. You get a little noise and it gradually, over the course of many, many months, gets louder and louder. But it happens so incrementally that you have no idea how bad it is.

Until someone gets in the car with you and says "Omygawd! What is that noise?" And you say, "Noise? What noise?"

So what's the lesson here?

Don't hit potholes. *or curb side*

Don't laugh. That is the lesson. How do you avoid potholes? Don't drive where the potholes are. And the potholes are mostly on city streets. So stay off city streets as much as you can.

You've heard people say that highway miles are easier on a car than city miles, and this is a major reason why. (Another reason is that you don't use up clutches and brakes on highways, like you do on city streets.) So, if you have a choice of two routes to get somewhere, take the one that's mostly highway, even if it's longer.

If you prevent the shakes, you'll eliminate the rattles.

The last piece of advice is *don't downshift*.

Don't. Other than the fact that it sounds good and makes you feel like an Indy 500 driver, downshifting is stupid. You downshift because you want to slow down. But that's what the brakes are for.

Why use the clutch, which costs $500 to replace, when you could be using the brakes, which cost $150 to replace? Plus, every time you downshift, you put more stress on those $800 worth of C-V joints.

You should downshift if you're driving down Mt. Kilimanjaro, because the brakes will fry if you apply them for a long time. Or if the brakes don't work. Or if it's an emergency and you have to stop ASAP.

But otherwise, use the brakes to brake.

THE CRITICAL YEAR

A funny thing happens on the way to the junkyard. We always see cars that are "hangin' in there pretty good" (or pretty well, if you're an English major).

And then something happens. It seems that almost overnight, it turns to junk.

A lot of people like to think that the manufacturer planned it that way—that everything will last for X years and then self-destruct.

Au contraire, Piston Puss!

What happens is not mechanical, it's psychological. The owner has reached the *critical year*. Sometime during the critical year, you subconsciously decide to kill your car. Who knows why? Maybe that sleazeball brother-in-law just got a new car and you're jealous. Maybe you got a raise and the money is burning a hole in your pocket. Whatever the reason, your subsconscious starts working on your car's demise. Here's what happens:

Someone bumps into you in the parking lot and dents a fender. You *know* what to do. You've read this book. You know that the cardinal rule is *fix everything*. But you don't get around to it.

A door handle falls off. Oh, well. It's in the back. You don't use that door very often anyway.

A neighborhood twerp scratches the side of the car with a nail.

A truck in front of you throws up a stone and cracks the windshield. What a pain. But it's not a big crack. You don't fix it.

You would have fixed all these things last year. But this year you don't. Then you skip a maintenance appointment.

Just little things. The car still runs. But there are a lot of little things.

You have reached the 'critical year.' Unchecked, you are headed straight for the boneyard. Do not pass "Go." Do not collect $200. In fact, do not pass the dealership. (They can solve all these problems. Come on in. 2.9 percent financing. New door handles. New windshield. New car smell. Only $15,000. You're done for!)

What to do, what to do.

This is serious. It's not called the critical year for nothing. It is critical. And it happens to us all. You must not succumb, my child. You must be strong. You must think of trips to Honolulu.

Here's what I recommend:

First, you must recognize what's happening. (And you will, since the previous paragraph has an embedded posthypnotic suggestion.)

Then go rent a car for about a week.

Then take your car in for a complete checkup (like the one you did when you bought it).

And fix everything.

Now, here's the good one: After everything is fixed, make the appointment to have your heap *painted*.

Right. You are going for the reincarnation. The second life for this baby. You are going to spend a grand or so and you are going to have a "new" car. Make sure the body shop gets rid of all the rust and dents. Then paint it a completely different color than it was before. Do whatever it takes to make it look like a completely different car. So that when you go to pick it up you'll have all the excitement of picking up a *new* car.

Ray: Yeah, sure. You're going to be real happy with an orange car with a blue interior.

This takes great courage. In the critical year, you will have lots of miles on the car. People will tell you that "anything could happen." Avoid these people. They are the children of Satan and will steal your soul. When confronted by them, go back and read Chapter Eight again. Carry this book around with you and ward off these people by waving Chapter Eight in their faces.

They will say, "You could spend all this money on the paint job and next week the transmission could need a rebuild." This is true. But a transmission rebuild does not cost $15,000.

Remember, if the car is basically sound (i.e., the body has not rusted away), it is *always* cheaper to fix it.

Do not succumb.

Repeat the mantra:

Waikiki Beach.

Waikiki Beach.

Waikiki Beach.

If this doesn't work, call the Critical Year Support Group Hotline: 1-800-Waikiki.

Ray: He's my brother and I love him, but he's nuts— he's really nuts.

INDEX